Why Do I [illegible]
Me The Way They Do?

The Autobiography Of Jefferson Evans

by Jefferson Evans and Glenn Ellis

The First Black Graduate Of The Culinary Institute Of America, 1947

Positive Records Period

I would like to dedicate this book to the world. I hope that somewhere, someone in the world reads this book and decides to treat the people they see a little better. Maybe one day, nobody will ever have to ask the question. ***Why do people treat me the way they do?***

WHY DO PEOPLE TREAT ME THE WAY THEY DO?

Table of Contents

FOREWORD

I'm honored to be included and participating with other great culinarians to write some words of thought to contribute to the memoirs of Chef Jefferson Evans, the first Black graduate in America maybe even the world of a major culinary institution. The first comment I have is that I believe and feel anyone who aspires to be a food historian should know this part of American Food History and many do not. In part, this is the demise of culinary education promoting diversity. There is also a deficiency in understanding of people inside and outside of the food industry of what it is like to go to a premier culinary institution as someone of color. So I encourage people to learn about the life and times of Jefferson Evans who I regard as the Jackie Robinson of Culinary Arts.

My story is a dim light in comparison to Chef Evans. He graduated the Culinary Institute of America in 1947. I graduated in 1989, over four decades later. I cannot begin to imagine the campus environment in which someone of color would have to endure. Albeit I can do my best at coming up with an assumption. Let me put this in perspective.

The CIA is without a doubt one of the premier culinary institutions in the world. Since its creation, the standards set for learning cooking fundamentals have set much of the standard within the world. Master Chefs are the instructors and the top faculty teaches everything from wines to service. It was my desire to compete with the best and that's exactly what I did.

My first few weeks at the start of landing at the school was quite an entry point. The school is on the Hudson River and the feel is one of a gothic place which makes sense because it was previously a Jesuit Monastery. As I entered the school for the first day It was clear to me, very clear to me that there were not a lot of people who looked like me. In fact, many hours passed by before I saw someone of color, needless to say, there was a look of shock for both of us when we saw each other. The very peculiar thing was that my expecting the common hello was met with looking away only after a nonverbal node of the head. Many days and weeks went by before I met all of the faces that looked like me; this was relatively easy because there were only a hand full of us. The teachers and faculty, for the most part, had a sense of professionalism, although some would confide in me that it was rare to have a student of color in their class. The environment and tone of the school were unmistakably European. Relative to other students I was already in the industry prior to attending culinary school. It's not a secret that I lied about my age to when I was 15 so I could start to work in a large restaurant with the big boys. By the time I was 21 and attending CIA I had already assembled my preliminary battle scars and so I was not prone to be intimidated by anyone. I think I can say this was very apparent in which I conducted interactions while a student there. Quite frankly I thought the social environment was toxic for me as a black student and so every chance I had I spent most of my time off campus socializing and making friends at other schools in the nearby area.

The light came on bright one day while in class with a chef instructor who was from South Africa. I had the privilege and rare solar eclipse of having another black student in the class with me. The attitude from the chef towards me as well as verbal comments were combative. I was actually told I was going to be broken. I think I laughed out loud but maybe in hindsight would have taken a different approach if I could turn back time. Psychologically speaking I felt threatened and I also realized that he knew If he pushed me over the line there was a likelihood we were going to have a sit down where only one of us were going to be getting up. At twenty-one years old I lacked some discipline towards diplomacy but people always got the point. I was seriously reactive to any attack or confrontation.

We were making sauces that day, and although I wasn't paying attention to what was anyone else's sauce creations but I could tell my brother was struggling a bit. The chef came over to his station and asked what he was doing. He said I was making a sauce that was met with two comments in which one was accurate and the other put everything into a new frame. The first comment was that the sauce was garbage. Common practice at the school was anything below perfection was called in fact garbage or worst. I was cool with that, the next comment not quite so. After trying to defend why maybe the sauce was less than par the chef then called him a Kaffir. There was an electric shock that shot up my spine, I don't know why but I felt at that moment two things. The first was the sorriest feeling for my fellow classmate and embarrassment. Although the comment was directed towards him I knew it was indirectly aimed at me. The second feeling was the fact I had a short menu of predetermined options if It was ever my turn to be humiliated in front of the class. Needless to say, I felt compelled to meet with him privately after class. I won't go into detail about this meeting but I can tell you there was a meeting of the minds. Not to be overlooked the student reported the incident and there was absolutely no reprimanding of any kind. That was the environment for someone of color.

This incident also was the catalyst for me to be more involved in improving the environment for students of color on campus. As a result, the Minority Cultural Society, an on-campus support group for students of color for supportive conversation and encouragement was formed. Unlike Chef Evans we were not alone. I also want to frame this message not in racism but in resiliency. Racism will always exist and is not a variable but resilient. Developing optimism and resiliency isn't about blind optimism.

It's a trait that that Chef Evans has developed that speaks volumes to people today. Imagine the grit necessary over 40 years ago to be a pioneer in American Food History by being not only the first Black graduate of CIA but the first the Black instructor of the second most prestigious school in the country, Johnson and Wales. This is the essence of courage the cornerstone of confidence and leadership. Even today there is an apparent lack of leadership for people of color in the culinary industry. That needs to not only improve but relatively change in order for young people to see themselves as successful agents of positive change for tomorrow. In his nineties, Chef Evans refuses to change his philosophy of It' that success is the by-product of success. Having the courage to see and meet life exactly as it is. Showing all of us how to choose (yes it is by choice) to learn how to respond to each adversity with confidence, hope and renewed vigor.

Alex Askew
Pres. BCAGlobal
CIA, 1989

FOREWORD

It is an honor to be a part of black culinary history exemplified in the following memoir you are about to read. Chef Jefferson Evans, for those who have had the privilege to meet him, has been such a powerful influence representing culinary education, perseverance of the same, and social mindfulness. The latter speaks echoing volumes to a black culinarian such as myself. After meeting Chef Evans my whole world/life was changed, partly due to the fact that I was in the culinary industry and also because I was a relatively young black man at the time. After reading his memoirs, hopefully, your world/life will be changed and you will embark on a journey to continue his legacy, passion for culinary arts, and the desire to help mentor other young black and minority young professionals.

Chef Evans and I share some similarities in our lives that are really significant to our relationship. First, Chef Evans was the first black graduate of the Culinary Institute of America (CIA) in 1947; my mother was born in 1947. Being raised by a single black woman in the 80's and 90's I was told a lot about what black folks had to go through during her time growing up, and in turn, she was told about what the generation that proceeded her had to go through. As I grew up, she told me something that her father told her growing up, "In order to be equal to white folks, you need to be 120% better....and when you are, they still won't acknowledge it". Secondly, when some minority students for Johnson & Wales University (JWU), one of the premier culinary institutions in the country and my alma mater, went to Connecticut to visit Chef Evans and hear about his life, he told them the very same thing! They were amazed, taken aback, and dumbfounded to hear how he and many other blacks were viewed and treated in this industry during his time coming up. They were also amazed to hear that Chef Evan had actually taught at JWU in the mid-late 70's as the first black culinary instructor.

Not too much was said about Chef Evans' time at JWU except that he only taught there for a year. Now, many of us, like myself, could gather from his recollection that it was a trying time for him like it was for myself. Having gone to JWU receiving an Associates in Culinary Arts, and Bachelors in Foodservice Management, and an MBA in Hospitality I knew the system well and after a while was not a fan. Where were all of the instructors or color? Where were the black culinary instructors? Throughout all of my culinary labs I did stellar work and received all B's; 89's!! Through that, I still received a recommendation from all of my chef instructors to be a teaching assistant in the prestigious Culinary Events department; because they knew I was good, but couldn't bring themselves to grant me the A that I deserved. I went on to be the first black teaching assistant in the department since its inception. After working my way up from teaching assistant to Special Project Coordinator in two years, and not without a lot of static, I was approaching my undergraduate graduation and faced with my next steps in life. Simultaneously, I had just had the honor of meeting Chef Evans and heard his story. My decision was made easy, and I decided to enroll in graduate school, continuing to work at JWU while pursuing my MBA; but how would I pay for it? I heard that there was Management Development Program (MDP) that would pay for 90% for your graduate tuition while making $35,000 per year. The only problem was our department never had MDP's in it, so I went to the dean of culinary arts at the time and requested that we implement the MDP in out department so that I could continue my education and work at the university. He told me, "Adam, we cannot circumvent the system just for you, you're going to have to find a way to pay for graduate school if that's what you want to do". That is exactly what I wanted to do and did. Three months later he circumvented the system for one of my Caucasian peers, creating a MDP slot in our department giving him everything that I had just recently requested; and I was 120% better. I didn't waiver, I continued on my journey getting promoted to assistant director and Director within the next two years.

During that time I, along with the first Student Chapter of the BCA (Bridging Culinary Arts) and JWU and in the country had the pleasure of honoring Chef Jefferson Evans, bringing together students and faculty from CIA and JWU to honor Chef Evans for his contribution to both institutions, the culinary industry, and to our lives. The idea coming from my dear friend and co-author of this forward, Chef Alex Askew, we were able to bring awareness and desire to many young culinarians of color. After fighting and clawing at success and the hunger to be great, this was my most memorable time at JWU. Knowing that I walked in the same halls, and took classes in the same classes that Chef Evans taught walked through and taught in gave me strength. It gave me the motivation to continue on. It reminded me that I am great, that I will succeed, and that no one can hold you down.

I am now the first black culinary instructor at Kennesaw State Universities Culinary Sustainability and Hospitality College in Kennesaw, Georgia.

Thank you, Chef Evans, for all that you have given us.

Chef Adam J. Joseph

From the co-author

I met Mr. Evans in August 2013. I was introduced to Mr. Evans by my cousin, Dwane. After spending some time with Mr. Evans, I learned that he had begun to write a book and had a desire to complete it. I offered to help him and this is the culmination of that effort. Mr. Evans gave the book its title and its overall theme. I tried to help tell the story as Mr. Evans gave it to me. Some of the stories come from his original manuscript and some are from recordings Mr. Evans made telling his stories for the last couple of years. I am honored to have been the recipient of history in the making and I only hope that I was able to capture the true essence of his stories. I will certainly take credit for any shortcomings found within. Mr. Evans has a joke of saying whether something is like Oak Street, which he considered the worst street in New Haven or like Hollywood. I hoped this book to be Hollywood, but if it is somewhere between Oak Street and Hollywood, I will be content.

Glenn Ellis

INTRODUCTION

My name is Baron George Poitier. I am the youngest grandson of Jefferson Evans. Today is December 27, 2014. I am 34 years old. I am joined here with my wife Christian who is also 34 years old. I have an 11-year-old daughter. She is the number one wedding gift I received, Jasmine Simone Rainbow. We have also our first miracle child, Isabella Joy Rainbow, born Sept 2012. We also are joined by Samuel Baron Poitier, my first boy born in Sept 2013. We had the wonderful pleasure of sitting with my grandfather as we always do. We currently live In Grand Prairie, Texas. We have been married for five years. Every time we come to Connecticut, we take the time to come out and sit with my grandfather who is a great man of wisdom and knowledge and insight. People have not always understood him and have probably wanted to change who he is, but his authentic self is his best self. He has much to give this world and much to give a person like me who is raising my own family and trying one day to be a great person and to set a precedent for my own children as he has set for me. He has always been a person of great integrity. He has always done exactly what he said he was going to do. As a man coming up one day wanting to be a man and a father and a husband, he was a great role model. He served as a great example of what true manhood really looked like. I appreciate him for that. Today being the anniversary of my grandmother passing, he is still pressing forward never letting anything stop him from doing what God has called him to do and what is in his heart to do. And that is to help people to make sure his life is better and better every single day by also making those lives around him like mine even better. So I just want poppy to know I love him and I'm telling to his face right now. I love him. He does my heart joy every time I see him and that's all we have.

My name is Stanley Dixon. I am the nephew of Uncle Jeff. I remember him from the sixties. I remember him from about the age of eleven or twelve. He used to take us out and show us a good time. I am here with my oldest son Timothy and my wife, Sheena. What we remember most is when my four children and I came from Arizona, I was in the navy. I went to officer training school in Rhode Island and Uncle Jeff and Aunt T. came to my graduation. I was always blessed by his presence there. It was a great experience and I loved them for coming. His life has been a testimony to many. Someone wrote me the other day and said your uncle is a great inspiration. He reminds me of Frederick Douglass, not in just the way he looked but in what he did, breaking down barriers and being the first black chef to graduate from the Culinary Institute of America. He then went back to be an instructor of that same institution. The establishment of the Jefferson Evans scholarship has been a blessing to many. We are proud to be a part of this family.

Chapter 1
The Early Years in Georgia

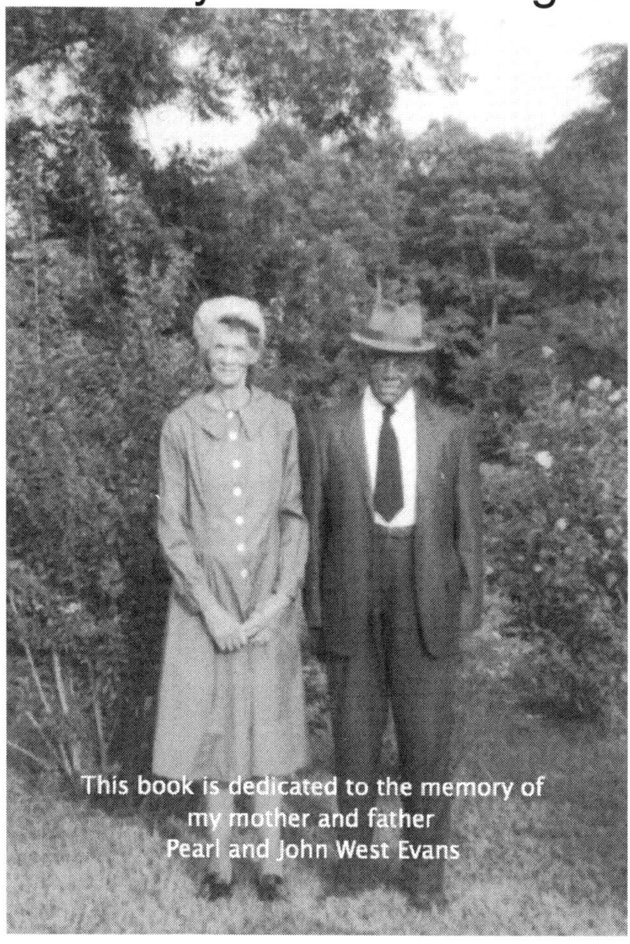

This book is dedicated to the memory of
my mother and father
Pearl and John West Evans

My name is Jefferson Evans. I was born June 2,1923. I would like to tell you stories about my life. In my story, I will ask this question many times. Why do people treat me the way they do? When I was about six months old my sister who is named Ann set my cradle on fire. Ann was born January 16,1922. She is a little more than a year older than me. So even though I can't remember it, I still have the scar on my right hand after 92 years to remind me. I do remember something that happened when I was about four or five years old. My brother Virtus who was born July 4, 1920, set the house on fire. We were living on a farm and we grew cotton. When we picked cotton we would store it in the house and on the porch. Now cotton is very soft. That day I was sleep on the cotton and my brother set the cotton on fire. The fire reached me and I jumped up and ran off the porch. My father was not home. A neighbor came running over and helped put out the fire. They took all the rest of the cotton out the house and put it in the yard in small piles. They poured water all over the fire. When my father came home, he saw all that cotton in the yard. Once he found out what happened, he beat my brother's butt. So even here early as a child, I have to ask the question. **Why do people treat me the way they do?**

In the fall we gathered the crops. I remember it was 1928. Our house was in bad shape, so my father decided to move. We moved five miles away. I was riding in the wagon and I bumped my head. On the way, we stopped by my mother's father's house, which was one mile away. My grandfather had two wives. I saw my mother's mother only once. That was my grandmother. I saw her when I was about five years old on my way to my new house. She looked like a white lady. She looked sick. That's all I remember. I never saw her again. I never even talked to her, never said a word. I don't know what happened to her. Being a little boy it always came to my mind, but I never said anything to my mother about it. My mother never talked about her at all. My grandfather had a big two family house with a porch all around it. He had a second wife that my mother called cousin Hattie. He had five children by cousin Hattie. She had one eye. She was evil looking. Some of Hattie's grandchildren lived on the plantation. They called her 'Grandma Hattie'. My mother told us that was not our grandmother. She said it was her cousin. I only saw my grandmother one time in my life.

When we got to our new house, it was a big barn, one big room. My father made it into four rooms. Later on, he built a dining room and kitchen. He also built stables and a barn for the horses, mules, cows and pigs. We had to clean up the land to start farming. My father had a lot of work to do, cutting trees, digging up stumps, burning bushes and cultivating the land. My father was a hard worker. Besides the stables for the animals, the barn for the tools, he had to build a fence around the place so the cows would not run away. My father built a house for the chickens, called a hen house, a house for the hogs, a blacksmith shop, a smokehouse and an outhouse. We had to find some water. We found a spring about two blocks from our house. We had to dig a hole near the spring. You had to build a box so the water from the hill would not run into it, but sometimes it did. Sometimes it would rain and the water would run down from the hill and the water would be muddy. We drank water sometimes that wasn't even clear, muddy water. One time my father was drinking some water and he got a fever. We thought he was going to die. We got scared but he passed over that. A neighbor across the street not too far from us had dug a well. At least two or three other people used water from his well.

Let me tell you about some of the things we had to do. We had about 200 chickens. That's why we needed a henhouse. On the farm, you have different animals. You have to treat your animals the same way you treat your family. I am going to start with the dog. A dog is a very important animal. He keeps the chickens out of the garden. He goes into the woods to help catch rabbits. At night when the moon is full of light, a man with his gun and dog go into the woods to catch a possum. The dog catches the scent of the possum. The dog runs after the possum and the man runs after the dog. So when the possum gets tired he runs up a tree and the dog stays there barking until the man catches up. The man sometimes is about a half mile away. Sometimes the possum is too fat so he cannot climb the tree. So he lays there and plays dead.

The next animal I am going to talk about is the chicken. The rooster is like the man. He runs after a hen which is a female and catches her and then he gets on top of her. I guess he can tell when a chicken is in heat. We made a hen house and the chickens went in there in the evening to sleep. We had about 200 chickens. Chickens eat mostly anything. They love corn and grain. When we were small we did not eat much chicken. We raised them to sell for money. My mother would look at the chicken and she might see one or two wet behind the butt, which meant they were sick. My mother would kill the chicken before he died. These would be the chicken we ate. When the preacher came over he would eat chicken and we would eat the chicken feet. Today it seems like you still see some of those sick chicken in the store that are being sold for cheap.

The hog is the next major animal on our farm. My family raised about 100 hogs at a time. The hog is an adult pig. The pig is a baby hog. We would put about five or six hogs each one by themselves to fatten up. We would feed him good. We put it in a pen where he could not move around and we would fatten it up. Then once it got fat enough, we would kill it and keep the meat to last throughout the winter and year. We sold the rest of the hogs and pigs for money.

Another very important animal on our farm was the cow. The bull is the male. The cow is the female. It is the same as a man and a woman. Every morning at 5:30 we got up and milked the cows. Sometimes we are half sleep. We kept cows in the barn. We sometimes had about 30 to 35 cows. We would sit down on the stool and start pulling the tit. Sometimes you may pull too hard and the cow kicked the milk pail over. You lost the milk and I didn't drink milk that day. The cow has four milk tits, two for the family and two for the calf. The boys in the family milked cows in the morning, in the afternoon the girls milked the cows. After you milk the cow you let the baby calf eat and then we separated the baby from the mother. If you do not separate the calf, you would have no milk. In the daytime, you let the cows out to eat grass. You have to watch those cows, cause they will break into the field and eat the corn. If you let them into a wild onion field, then you would have some horrible milk, milk you can't even drink. We had to build a fence around our land which was about ninety acres. There was a time when our cows got out the fence. I remember a man next door, he was about the same age as my father. He had kids our age that played with us until they were about thirteen. Then we didn't see them anymore. Anyway, this man cut the fence and drove our milk cow on his property. We got our money from the milk cow. My mother made butter and sold it along with milk from the cow. She also fed the babies with that milk so that cow was the main cow.

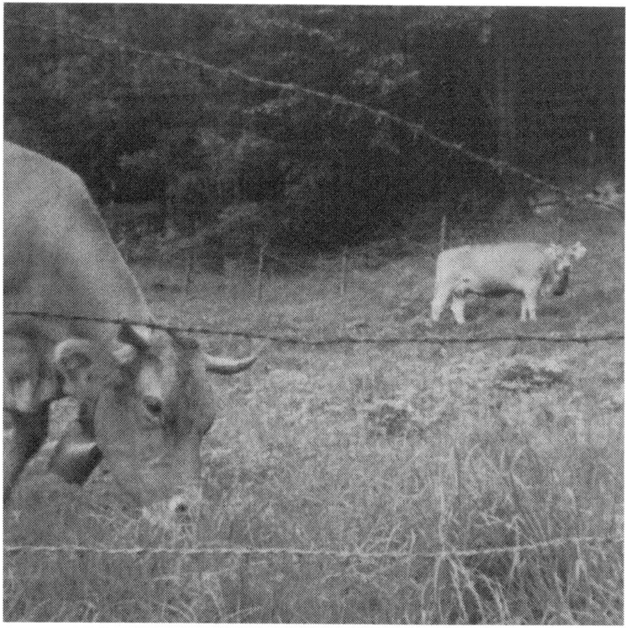

The man put the cow into his stall and then came over to us and said we had to pay to get the cow back. If daddy didn't have five dollars we wouldn't have a milk cow. So daddy had to sell a pig, sell chickens, eggs, something to get that cow back.

The horse, the mule, and the ox do the

heavy work on the farm. They are a very good help on the farm. These animals pull the wagon and help plow the land. Plowing is turning over the soil. Work on a farm is a hard job. I started working on the farm when I was five years old. My father had me in the field working and holding on to the plow, while he was plowing. When you are that small you learn fast. I wanted to do what my dad was doing. I was a big boy for my age. At the age of six my father gave me a plow. He hitched the ox bull to the plow. He gave me the plow and the bull attached to the plow and put me in this big field and said go plow. I grabbed the handle of the plow and the bull pulled me and the plow across the field. When we came to the end of the field, the bull stopped and I stopped. The bull knew the difference between a man and a child. He went up and back but when he got back, I guess he said it's too hot out here. He went into the shade and would not move anymore. I tried to get him to go but he would not go, so I laid down and went to sleep. My father came and saw me sleeping and the bull resting and laughed at me. My father trained me and by the age of ten, I was as good as my father. We had a big orchard that had peaches that came in April and May. We had a tree that produced apples in May and then again in August. My father was a tough man. He used to always say don't let the sun catch you home. We used to be up early waiting for the sun to come up so we could see how to plow.

The work started in March. You started turning up the soil to get it ready for planting. We planted cotton, sweet potatoes, corn, wheat, oats, cabbage, collard greens and peanuts. So at the time I moved to this farm at the age of five, it was my dad, John West Evans, my mom, Pearl Evans, my brother Virtus, my sister Anna, and me, Jeff, my sisters Mattie and Barbara and at that time Ella was the baby. At that time my father bought 90 acres of land. This was October 1928. Our house was an old house, built in the 1800's. When we got there, no one was living there. There was another old house in the back of us in the woods. We used wood from that house to build rooms for our house, which at first was just one big room like a barn. My dad made this into four rooms. In it, we built two fireplaces, one on each side of the house. We cleared the land because you could put wheat in the ground in October, so we could eat bread the next year. In about March you could see it growing and by July you could cut the wheat and grind it to make flour to make bread. Each year we would clear more land and plant more corn, more cotton, more wheat, more potatoes, more everything and then there were also, more children. We ended up with 11 children.

Next to our farm, was a white farmer and across the street was a black farmer. We had to walk three miles to school. In our village, there were two white families with six children.

The bus came and picked them up to go to school. There was a time when there was only one child and the bus picked him up while we walked to school. It was awful. Sometimes the bus would ride by us and we would wave. My mother was a teacher. She went to college in Atlanta, Spellman college. Every year our family grew larger. My mother taught us how to read. We started school in October.

The white schools started in September. We finished school in March. The white schools finished in June. Even though we registered in October we still had to gather the crops. We had to put food away for the family and for the animals for the winter. It took us until December to do all this before we could really start school. In March we had to start tilling the land so we had to stop going to school.

We learned the 3 r's…reading, 'riting' and 'rithmetic. Every morning we had to get up at five if we wanted to go to school.

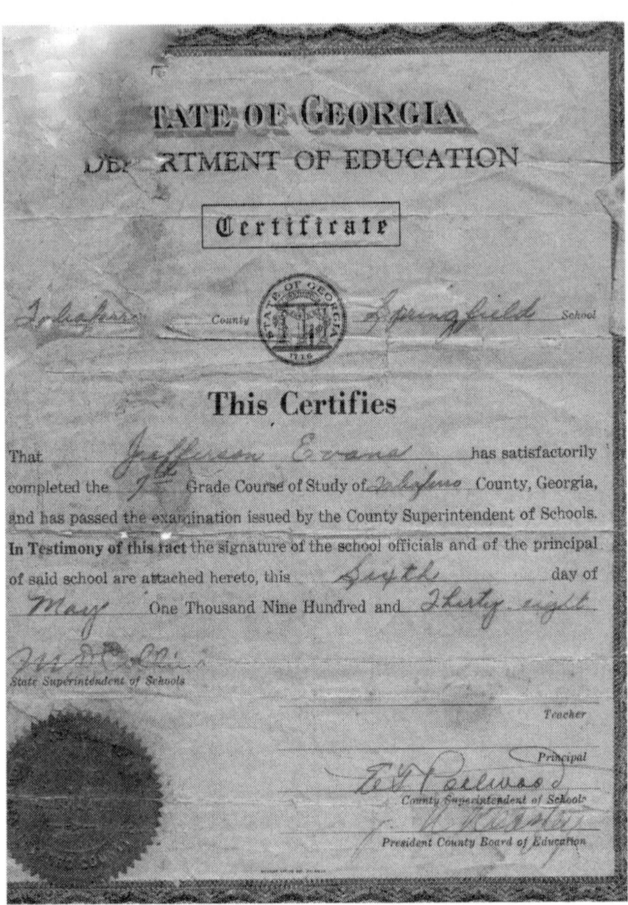

TATE OF GEORGIA

DE RTMENT OF EDUCATION

Certificate

Jefferson County Springfield School

This Certifies

That Jefferson Evans has satisfactorily completed the 7th Grade Course of Study of Jefferson County, Georgia, and has passed the examination issued by the County Superintendent of Schools. In Testimony of this fact the signature of the school officials and of the principal of said school are attached hereto, this Sixth day of May One Thousand Nine Hundred and Thirty eight

State Superintendent of Schools

Teacher

Principal

County Superintendent of Schools

President County Board of Education

We had to get breakfast. We had to feed the horses and milk the cows. At night my sisters milked the cows. We had to walk a couple of miles to go to school. We had to go by my grandfather's house every day. The school was on my grandfather's land.

He had about 500 acres. One day me and my brother Virtus asked our father why did we have to say mister to our white neighbor but his kids just called you Hat. My father didn't answer us. He didn't want to get into that kind of stuff. So we decided that we wasn't going to say mister to that neighbor. One day we was on our way to school and he was out plowing and we had to pass by him. We walked by him and we said "hello Teet." He got so mad. He came over and told our father. He was hot. Teet Edwards, that was his name.

I remember in 1930, it rained just about all summer. It was too wet to plant. Grass took over everything and we lost money. We lost our farm but we still lived there. The way it worked, in March we had to borrow money to start over. We planted a lot of cotton, because with cotton you get cash money. With it, it helped pay what we borrowed in March. We sold chickens, eggs, milk, corn, wheat, hogs, cows and we got more money. Say you pick 1500 pounds of cotton which is a bale of cotton. You got five cents per pound for the cotton and three cents per pound for the seeds. In a good year, you could make 10 to 15 bales of cotton. Some years were good, some years were bad. Every Saturday people in the city would buy from the farmers like us. They bought chickens, eggs, watermelon, corn, wheat, everything we grew, people would buy it. Every year we worked, worked, worked, worked and on these Saturdays we got paid for our work.

My father and mother were church going people. They loved the Lord. They prayed all the time. My father and mother told us if you don't study, you would grow up stupid. They told us, go to school. They would say you will never be anything without school. They would say this over and over. They would use my father's cousin, Mr. Jones as an example. Mr. Jones was a smart man who I guess finished college. He was head of the agricultural bureau in our district. So we heard about Mr. Jones all the time. He was a good talker in the church also. I left home at the age of 16. I never forgot what they said about education. My mother and father were good people. They taught us how to live, how to work, how to pray. My father would always say, "white people don't like slow people, they like smart people." They told us to go to church. They told us not to go into bad places, places where people drink. They told us never gamble, never drink beer and wine.

At 12 years I saw everything that happened on a farm. I did everything a person could do on a farm, starting with getting up at 5am, feeding horses, cows, chickens, hogs, milking cows, knowing how to shoe horses and mules and working in the blacksmith shop. I learned how to save food for the winter months. In October we started gathering crops. We put away food for us and for the animals. We put away food like hay, corn, oats, wheat and potatoes. We canned our fruits and vegetables. We made soap, syrup, wine. We made hills covered with straw to store our sweet potatoes. After we gathered the crops, we would begin to put wheat in the ground around November. The wheat stayed in the ground throughout the winter and in March or so, you start seeing it growing up, turning green like grass. In about May or June, it grew up with seeds. Then we would cut it up and wrap it into bales. We had to separate the seeds from the wheat or as the bible says the wheat from the chaff. We didn't throw any of it away. With the husk, we made gram bread. We made flour and other things from the seeds. We saved the hay for the animals. We didn't throw anything away with the corn either. We chopped up the cobs of the corn for the horses and they loved it. I remember somewhere before the '40's, I was around 12 or 13, my brothers and my father collected scrap iron. Japan was buying as much iron as they could. We had these large steel boilers and someone came and cut them up into pieces and we sold that too.

In 1940 my uncle had a liquor steel. He was my father's youngest brother. His name was Charlie. His liquor steel was deep in the woods. He put liquor into jars and sold it wherever he could. People would come to his house and buy it. He even brought it to the church and sold it outside, not directly, but near enough to the church. He would bring it to us when we were sick and give us a tablespoonful with sugar and we would get better. Sooner or later the prohibition people came and arrested Charlie and put him in jail. They tore down the liquor steel. They charged him a hundred dollars, but he couldn't pay it. My daddy helped him get out on bond. Then my uncle decided to leave town and I went with him to help. I was about sixteen. We left one Friday night. We got on a train to go to Washington.

Chapter 2

Living In D.C.

When we got to D.C., a friend of ours from Georgia met us at the train station. He helped us find a room. We found a room on 71st St., a big room that costs two dollars and 50 cents a week.

Soon we went out to look for a job. I went to the employment office. They wanted to know what I could do. I told them I could do anything. The man said he had a dishwashing job. I said, "I'll take it." I went to work in a restaurant. I made eight dollars a week, working twelve hours a day, seven days a week. I came home that night and I was happy.

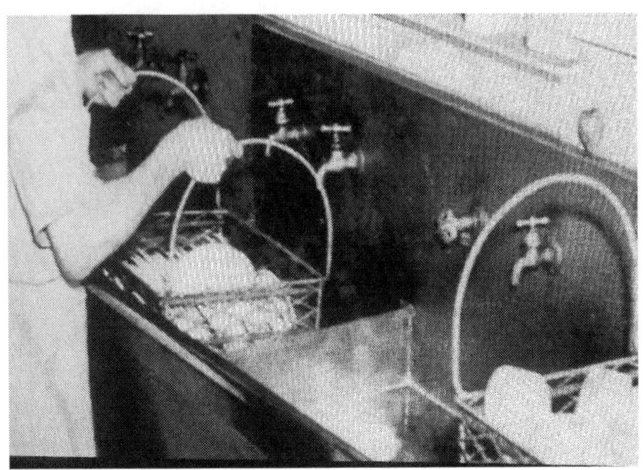

My uncle found a job building sidewalks with a company called Bencarte and Cement. That was hard work. He worked for six months and saved 100 dollars that he sent home to pay his debt. My uncle left and went back to Georgia, but I stayed in D.C.

I remembered my father saying, go to church, go to school and so I enlisted in night school. I wanted to learn a trade. I wanted to work on automobiles and other machines. I started night school. It was three nights a week. I went one week. I couldn't take it, along with working. I went looking for another job. I found one with the same hours making twelve dollars a week. I worked there for a while, but I wanted to make more money. I found a job working with a man helping him build houses for fifty cents an hour. I worked there for a while. Next, I got a job at the Pentagon building in Arlington, Va. This kid got me a job at the Pentagon. His uncle was in charge. They didn't give him a job but they gave me a job. It was a plain figure with five sides. I saw the first side getting built. I was one of the first people helping when the building began. When I started working there I was making eighty-seven and a half cents per hour. I worked there for about eight months. It was outside work and it was hard work. I felt it was too cold in D.C. in the winter.

At the Pentagon, my boss was a black man. He was married but he had no kids. He became my best friend and he treated me like his son. While I was working there, I gave him money every week to save for me. When I needed money to send home, he would give me what I needed. While I was working with him, we went to church every Sunday. I was young and good looking. I went out with him and his girl and I met girls also. So sometimes we went out together. By the time I quit my job working for him, I had given him a lot of money to save for me. My next job was at the Navy Department's message pool in D.C. We delivered messages all over the city to different departments. This was an inside job. It was a clean job and I had to dress up every day. I had to look good, just the kind of job that I wanted with lots of girls. I still saw my boss at church every Sunday. We talked, I still went to his house and we still went out together.

My boss still had my money that he was keeping for me. The money he had for me was about 250 dollars. One day when I saw him at church, I asked him for my money. He said okay. He told me to come to his house at six o'clock in the morning before I go to work. That same Sunday he sent a man to my house, just as it was getting dark. I was sitting on the porch when he came up. I knew this man from work. He asked me to walk with him to the park. I didn't feel like leaving my house, but he pleaded with me to walk with him to the park. I still said no. He was at my house for about a half and hour. I lived on a one-way street and while I was sitting there, a man driving a 1937 Plymouth came by my house. I recognized the man. He had been in jail for killing somebody. When I saw him, I began to think about my boss saying he was going to give me the money in the morning. Here this man is asking me to walk with him to the park and here this guy who is a killer is driving by my house. So I went upstairs. I live on the third floor. I asked God to tell me what these men are trying to do to me and went to bed. While I was in bed, God told me they wanted to kill me.

That morning I got up at 5 o'clock and I walked eighteen blocks to my boss's house to get the money that he said he would give to me. His wife greeted me at the door. She was glad to see me. My boss was in the kitchen getting ready for work. He came in the living room with a bag in his hand. I thought it was his lunch. He said hi and had the bag near his face. I was sitting on the sofa. He removed the bag from his face and said, "let's go." We talked and walked for seven blocks to a corner where I would be catching my bus to go to work. I saw my bus coming and I said to him,

"I'll see you tonight," and I walked across the street. As I stepped to the curb, he called me and I turned around. He said, "you asked for it, now you got it." He was holding the bag and he shot me through both knees. I fell to the ground. Across the street, a policeman was getting off the trolley car and he saw what happened. My boss told the policeman that I had a gun. The policeman came over and patted me down while I laid on the ground. He told my boss I did not have a gun. I went to the hospital and my boss went to jail. They put a cast on my left leg because the bullet went through the bone in the left leg. The bullet went through the meat in the right leg so I didn't have a cast on that one. Here is the question I said I would be asking throughout my story. **Why do people treat me the way they do?**

I stayed in D.C. for about a month before going back to my home in Georgia. I had been away for about four years. I stayed in Georgia for a while and then I went back to D.C. My sister Ann came to Washington. She got a job in a drug store. She was my favorite sister. When we were young one day on the way to school, I wanted to eat my lunch before we got to school and she didn't want to give it to me. I wanted to eat my biscuit that my mother gave me. My sister didn't take no junk. She hit me over the head with the lunch bucket. My father was two miles away and he said he heard the bang. Anyway, the drug store where she worked like most drug stores sold food. She used to feed me and I didn't pay for the food. Now the boss used to look over there where I was sitting at the counter and he didn't say anything about it. One day he came to me as I was going out. I guess he got tired of me and he asked me did I pay for that food. He said don't come in there no more and I drew back and hit him and knocked him on the floor. He was a fat man. Then I ran and ran. At first, I didn't go home. I went to another district. I never went back in there because I was scared he would call the cops.

Soon I went into the army.

At that time they were accepting just about everybody, even if you were sick. Everybody was going to have to fight the Japanese.

I never left the United States.

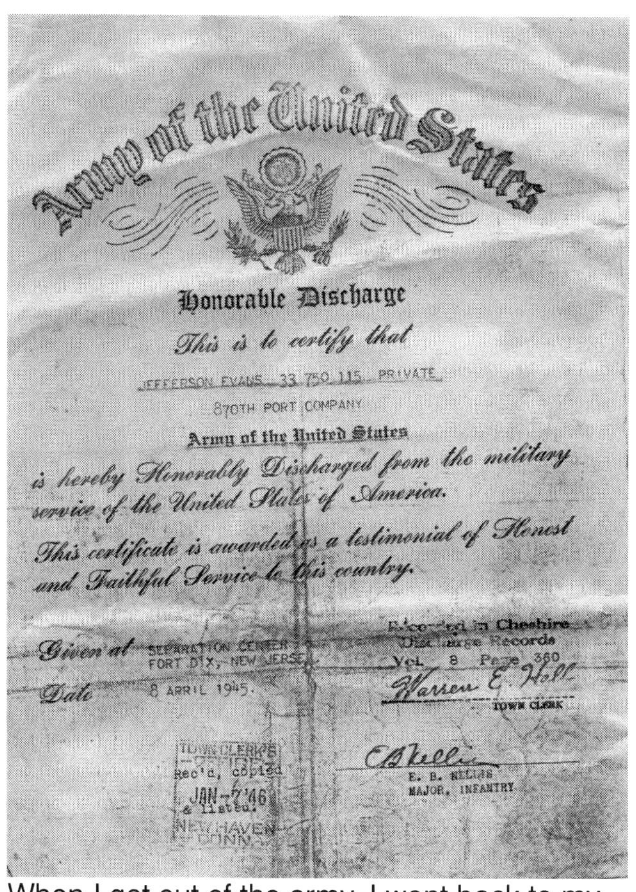
Army of the United States

Honorable Discharge

This is to certify that

JEFFERSON EVANS 33 750 115 PRIVATE

870TH PORT COMPANY

Army of the United States

is hereby Honorably Discharged from the military service of the United States of America.

This certificate is awarded as a testimonial of Honest and Faithful Service to this country.

Given at SEPARATION CENTER FORT DIX, NEW JERSEY

Date 8 APRIL 1945.

Cheshire Records
Vol. 8 Page 360
Warren E. Holt
TOWN CLERK

TOWN CLERK'S
Rec'd, copied
JAN-7'46
& listed.
NEW HAVEN
CONN.

E. B. NELLIS
MAJOR, INFANTRY

When I got out of the army, I went back to my old job at the Navy Department as a messenger in Admiral King's office. I went there for a few months. When I was leaving the army, they had given me a book about the college, Yale in Connecticut. I said to myself, "let's go to Yale in Connecticut." I got on the train and I came to Connecticut.

Chapter 3
The Move To New Haven, Ct.

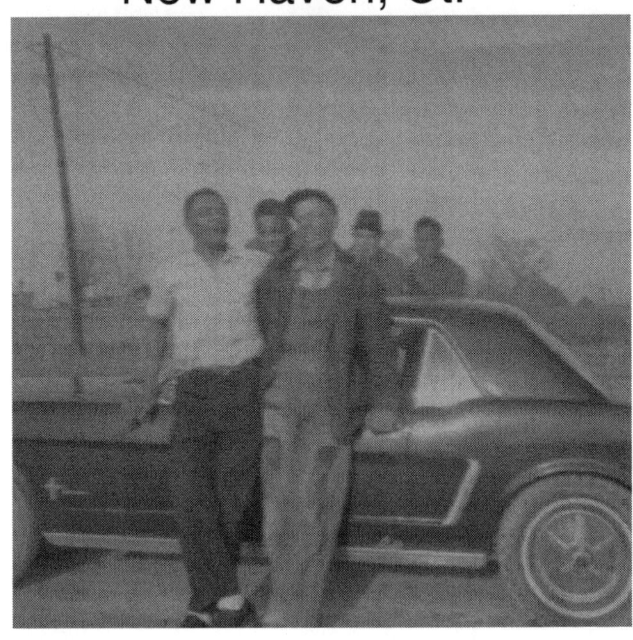

I got on a train that stopped in New York and then traveled on to Connecticut. I got off in New Haven, Connecticut. At the train station, I caught a cab. I asked the cab driver to go to a black hotel. The taxi driver came by Yale on the way to Dixwell Ave, where he brought me to the Nelson Hotel. I went in to get a room and I met Mr. Nelson, the owner of the hotel. The owner of the hotel also owned a barber shop. At the barber shop, I met another man named Eddie Nelson, who was close to my age. I told him I wanted to go to Yale. He was happy for me. The next day I went down to Yale to register.

I didn't realize what I had gotten myself into. While I was in Georgia, I never went to high school. All I studied was the three Rs, reading, 'riting and 'rithmetic. I went down to Yale for four days in a row to take the examination. I failed. Then I went looking for a job while I was still living at the hotel.

When I first came to New Haven, the first thing I did was look for black people. That's how I ended up at the Nelson Hotel. At that time there were about 400 black people in New Haven. They lived mostly on Dixwell Avenue, Orchard Street, Henry Street, Webster Street and Goffe Street, in that area.

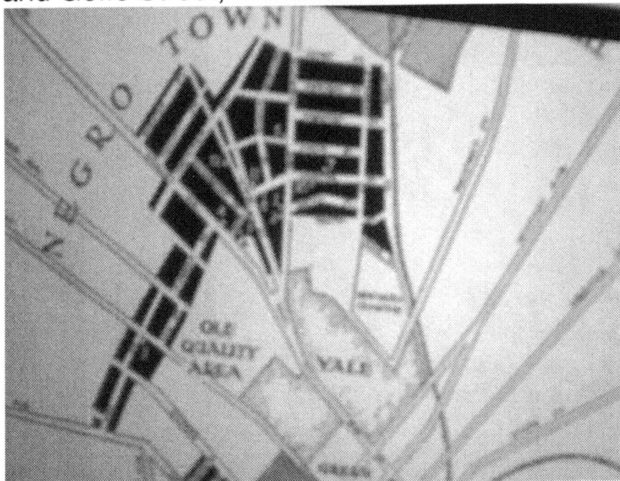

A few lived on Oak St. My wife and her family lived on Oak St. My wife was named Otelia. I met her in Philadelphia. There were a lot of Jewish people and Jewish-owned businesses in that area. In the Goffe St. area there were a lot of black-owned businesses. A big black man by the name of Frank Vincent lived on Goffe Street, but he owned a gas station on Oak St. He weighed about 250 pounds. I washed cars for him. He liked me. Frank was a great man. He had a brother named George and a cousin named Joe Ming. His family was on the ball. Like I said there were a lot of black businesses in the Goffe St area. There was a tea room and clubs. My cousin owned a dry cleaning business. There were stores, a pool room and there were black people owning trucking businesses. A lot of people lived in the Elm City Housing. At that time that was progress, better living, better houses. A black person owned a beautiful club on Willow St. named Lillian's Paradise. My wife used to sing there.

My sister Ella, My wife and I, My sister Ann

In the downtown area, places like the First National Bank, Sears Roebuck and Childs Restaurant reminded me of being down south because they were segregated.

After I failed my exams at Yale, my friend

Nelson wanted to make me a barber. I said no. Soon after trying out at Yale, I got a job working downtown at a restaurant called Chili's. It was owned by a Greek man, Mr. Chili. I became a dishwasher there. During that time my Nelson introduced me to Paul Kelley, a Navy man, who had just come home. Paul was married and had three children. He had no job so I got him a job at Chili's. He worked the night shift and I worked the day shift. One day I asked Paul to work my shift and his shift for two days. I took two days off and when I got back Mr. Chili fired me. He said that I made that boy do all the work. The next day I started culinary school, known as the Culinary Institute of America.

At that time I was living on Goffe Street and the school was over on State Street. That was in 1946. It was the first school of its kind in the country.

While I was going to school, Nelson and I bought a truck. If you had a truck, you could make money. We did all kinds of jobs. Most people heat with coal. When they clean out the stove, they take the ashes and put it in the cellar. People want you to clean out the cellar. There was no oil burner. You put the coal directly in the furnace. Whenever I was not in school, we went around to places like the city dump picking up scrap iron, whatever we could find. Nelson and I were just like brothers. Soon Nelson and I started a moving company called the Red Ball Express Truck Company. We had three trucks. Mr brother in law sold me a 1928 Chevrolet truck. That Chevrolet was a great truck. It was strong. My main truck was a 1931 Ford. That's the one we had the sign painted on. The Red Ball Express.

Jeff and Eddie Nelson

We received contracts from Yale Furniture Company to deliver furniture. This was during times when I was in school and Nelson was working as a barber. So we hired a driver to deliver the goods. His name was Amos. The driver went to the store to pick up the furniture to deliver. However, when the driver reached his destination, something was missing. A mattress was missing. That was the end of that job with Yale Furniture, but we kept the driver. We sent him on another job. He was crossing the bridge in Middletown and he turned the truck over and knocked out a street light. We had no insurance so it cost us $219. When I got out of school, I started driving myself. We went all the way to Springfield, Massachusetts to pick up furniture and bring it to New Haven. For our trip, the owner gave us a bad check, so we never got paid. We didn't know anything about a check. The check was for about forty dollars. With all of these problems, we did not stay in the moving business long. We made a few dollars with the truck. There was a guy who had a big truck. He used to go to all the dumps in Connecticut. He bought the dump in Milford. He was a black man. After World War II he was picking up things like cast iron and tin. If you get into the right place you could make a fortune in a day. Well, we went to his place in Milford. It was locked up. Me and my partner, we decided to get up at 4 o'clock in the morning and go there. We were going to go in there before he got there, but it was locked. We jumped over the fence. We went over there and start picking up the stuff that was laying down in the dumps. The police came in there and they took us to administration in Middletown. When we got there the man in charge said you can't go to that dump. The man bought the dump for $5000. He's the only one who can go in there and pick stuff. They let us go.

I walked to school every day. I walked past the restaurant that I was fired from. Mr. Chili, the man who fired me would be standing outside the restaurant on Church Street. He saw me and asked me where I was going. I told him I was going to cooking school and that I wanted to be a cook. Mr. Chili told me that when I finished school, he would give me a job. Every day as I was coming by the restaurant he would call me in and give me breakfast. Next to his restaurant was a restaurant called Lips. Down the street was another restaurant called Child's Restaurant. I never saw any black people in either of these restaurants. As I said, Mr. Chili was a Greek man and he did not care who came into his restaurant, but the other restaurants were segregated. In 1947, I graduated from the Culinary Institute of America, officially becoming the first black graduate of this institution.

After I graduated from the culinary school, Mr. Chili kept his promise and gave me a job. My hours were from 10am-7pm. I worked for him for about two years. I wanted to learn more about the restaurant business. I found a job in Milford at the Red Lobster. It was a classy Italian restaurant, just what I wanted. I wanted to learn how to cook Italian food. When I got there the owner asked me where I worked. I told him Chili's in New Haven. He looked down at that type of restaurant. Then he told me I can be the dishwasher with the hours of 730pm to 12am. I said I'll take it. The next day I went to Red Lobster and the boss said he had nobody washing dishes during the day. When I walked into that kitchen, I could have died. When I saw all those dishes, I stood there for a while and looked. He said this is the job. I thought about what my father had said to me as a boy growing up. He said nothing came easy. I started washing dishes by hand. I did that every night for one week. The next week the boss told me he was going to move me up to the broiler, cooking lobster. That's what I wanted. I worked there for two years. I did everything, cooked, cleaned floors and washed dishes. I worked hard at everything I did. I still worked my regular job at Chili's from 10am to 7pm. Eventually, the boss at Chili's heard I had a part time job and he dismissed me from my regular job. Besides attending the Culinary Institute of America, I went to other schools. As I said, the government wanted to take care of us. You could go to school as many times as you want. They paid you to go to school. I graduated from Modern School of Hairdressing. That was on Goffe Street.

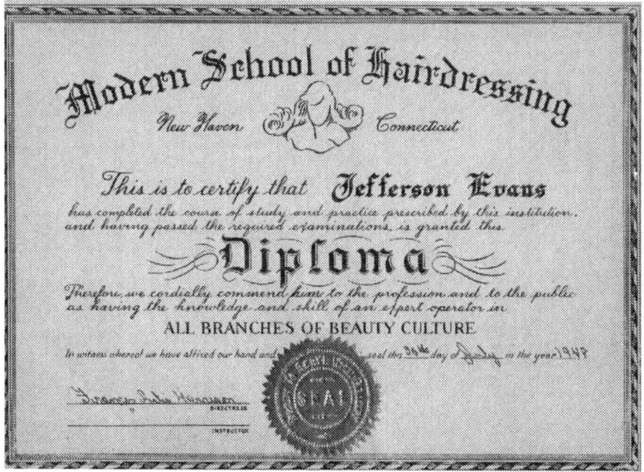
Modern School of Hairdressing

New Haven Connecticut

This is to certify that Jefferson Evans has completed the course of study and practice prescribed by this institution, and having passed the required examinations, is granted this

Diploma

Therefore, we cordially commend him to the profession and to the public as having the knowledge and skill of an expert operator in

ALL BRANCHES OF BEAUTY CULTURE

SEAL

DIRECTRESS

INSTRUCTOR

I went to correspondence school. I took up mechanics, oil burning.

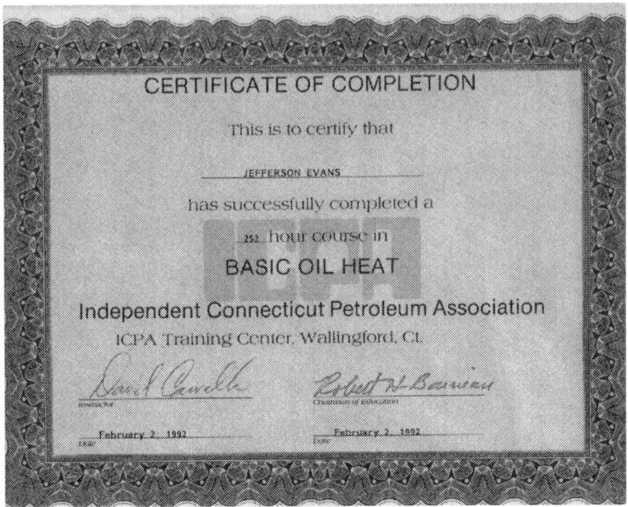

CERTIFICATE OF COMPLETION

This is to certify that

JEFFERSON EVANS

has successfully completed a

252 hour course in

BASIC OIL HEAT

Independent Connecticut Petroleum Association

ICPA Training Center, Wallingford, Ct.

Instructor | Chairman of Education

February 2, 1992 Date | February 2, 1992 Date

I went to real estate school. I decided you had to have more than one trade to live under the capitalist system.

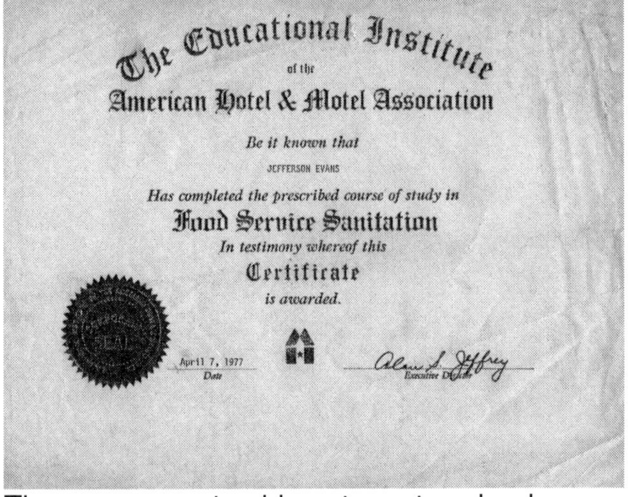

The Educational Institute of the American Hotel & Motel Association

Be it known that

JEFFERSON EVANS

Has completed the prescribed course of study in

Food Service Sanitation

In testimony whereof this

Certificate

is awarded.

April 7, 1977 Date

Executive Director

The government paid me to go to school because I had been in the army.

WINE INSTITUTE

Certifies that

Jefferson Evans

has completed its prescribed non-technical course in Wines, including Wine History, the Economic Importance of Wine, Wine Growing, Wine Classifications, Types and Uses, the Care and Handling of Wines, and the Essentials of Wine Selling. The recipient has successfully passed all examinations thereon and is hereby awarded this

CERTIFICATE OF MERIT

Signed and sealed at San Francisco, California

Endorsed:

CHAIRMAN — WINE ADVISORY BOARD

PRESIDENT — WINE INSTITUTE

SECRETARY-MANAGER — WINE INSTITUTE

I remember a time I was driving home at night. At this time I had no job. I was stopped for speeding. They had changed the rules of the road. I had to pay twenty-one dollars. Soon after I got this job in Milford painting. The boss was from Florida. I guess he understood black people. He said I got thirty painters. He said I will give you this job. He said mind your own business and work. I said thank you. I was working with this white boy. I was a guy who worked. They were building new houses after World War II and everything was getting good. Now I didn't know the boss was watching us paint. They always put me up to the top of the house. I was on the scaffold. I didn't care what section I was working in. I kept going and got to the section where the other guy was working. He wasn't doing much of nothing. The boss came in there, he started hollering. Oh God, I almost fell off the ladder. It scared me, but he wasn't hollering at me, he was yelling at the other guy. He was calling him names, you so and so, you haven't done nothing. I just kept working. I don't know if he fired him or not. Then the rain started. Now, all the white guys they could still work inside, but I had to work outside. With all the rain I couldn't work. So I quit that job. I worked one week. Painting is working outside. When it rains there is no work. Then I got a job at Rolling Mill in Waterbury. That was hard work. I worked there for a year. Then I decided to get a job in the field I loved, cooking. I said I got to get a job that I love in the restaurant business again. I said I'm a chef. I had to make myself believe that I was a chef. I put an ad in the newspaper. It read like this. "First class chef looking for a job. I love to work and will work hard." The ad costs twenty-five cents.They said I was too young, so I had to raise my age up. I said I was thirty. I went all over New Haven. One owner at a place I went said, "I would hire you, but you may be like the people I hired in the 1930's."

He said black people steal. This restaurant was on Chapel St. There were a lot of restaurants on Chapel St. in New Haven.

I went to another restaurant named Jacko's. It was widely known. It was near Yale. I was hired at Jacko's. While I worked at Jacko's, I met a few famous people. I met Governor Lodge from Connecticut and I met the governor from Massachusetts. The man I met who stood out the most was the football coach at Yale. His name was Herman Hickman. At Christmastime, this man sent me a Christmas card. The card has 500 names on that card. Now the owner Jacko was well known as a prize fighter. He acted like a bully. I said something to him he did not like. He invited me outside. I went outside and he put up his fists. I put up my fists. He turned around and went back inside. He did not want to hurt me. I left that job the next day.

At that time I was living in Elm Haven Housing on Webster Street. It was 1950. I had no job and my wife was pregnant with her third child. The first child Bunardy was born while we lived on Oak Street. The second child Dale was born while we were living In Elm Haven Housing on Webster Street. Calvin was the first boy. He was born in 1951. That was the last one. Three is enough. When I lost my job, my wife was ready to kill me. She had planned to go to Virginia. We had fifty dollars in the bank. She took it all out. My wife had our son shortly after she came home from burying her father. I had gotten a part time job working at the Goffe St. Spa. After work, I would work on my truck I bought called the Red Ball Express. We lived in Elm Haven for about nine years. It was an improvement, advancing toward perfection.

I did a lot of things since I left Jacko's

restaurant. My next job was at the Veteran's hospital in West Haven, Ct. I stayed a few weeks. Then I went to see this guy in Meriden. There were two brothers and a brother in law. I told him how much money I needed to make. He started me off at 125 dollars a week, twelve hours a day, seven days a week. I worked hard. I did great work. The restaurant was called Lord Cromwell. Upstairs in the restaurant there was a black fellow living there and working there. As time went on, business got good. I worked there for a year. Then the boss decided to hire someone. He said he was going to give the guy 50 dollars from the 125 he was giving me. So now he was going to give me 75 dollars. I left that night. I didn't say anything. That was Sunday night. The next morning I got up and went to the railroad station down in New Haven. This Greek fellow hired me right away. The Greeks were always nice, but this guy didn't want to spend any money. The stove there wouldn't close. We had to put a stick there to close the stove. I was on the grill cooking meat, bacon and all that stuff. I had been there for three days. The man wanted to know how I knew so much. I was cooking, cutting meat, doing everything. This day I was very busy so I was in a hurry and the door on the stove came down. When the door fell I had catch myself and so my hand fell right on that hot stove, right on the grill. I said to myself I'm quitting this job. I'm not going back there no more. All down there were restaurants, a wholesale place, a meat place. We had a mayor of New Haven, Richard Lee who changed the view of the whole world. He started redevelopment. He tore down a lot of things, the black neighborhood and the businesses there. Downtown, a lot of places, he tore down. He started redevelopment. He got a lot of money from the government and started rebuilding things. That was good I guess. Well, that same Wednesday, the guy from Lord Cromwell called me back. I told my wife that I wasn't going back to the railroad station anymore. She told me you just can't keep a job. I told her they don't treat me right. I told her to come with me to Meriden. I had been working there for about a year. I remember when I first got the job from him, he was telling me he needed a good man. I had sat in the office talking for about an hour. He said well Jeff, I'll call you, I'll let you know tonight. He said he would talk to his partner and let me know. I knew right then, he never was going to call me. I said to him, "you can go to New York, you can go to China, you can go to Tokyo, you can go anyplace in this world, but you are never going to find a man like me." Then he said, I'll give you the job. During that time I made him a lot of money. When my wife went with me, he met me in the yard. He said I don't like you but I'll give you the job. You didn't do this and you didn't do that. I said to him, "Mickey, I bring my wife out here with me and you embarrass me. I don't want the job" and walked away. He came running to my car. "Hey Jeff, come back, come back." I had told him he would have to give me the same 125 dollars with a day off, eight hours a day. He told me to start work tomorrow. I stayed with him a couple more years. When I quit, he got mad, did everything, cussed me out, because I was one of the best. He knew that. Over the years he would call me, wanting me to help him out. There was a time I was teaching and I went to help him. He said I had helped him out a lot of times. I quit because I got a job close to home. I got a job at Reilly's. I worked for Reilly's for ten years.

Chapter 4
Reilly's Restaurant

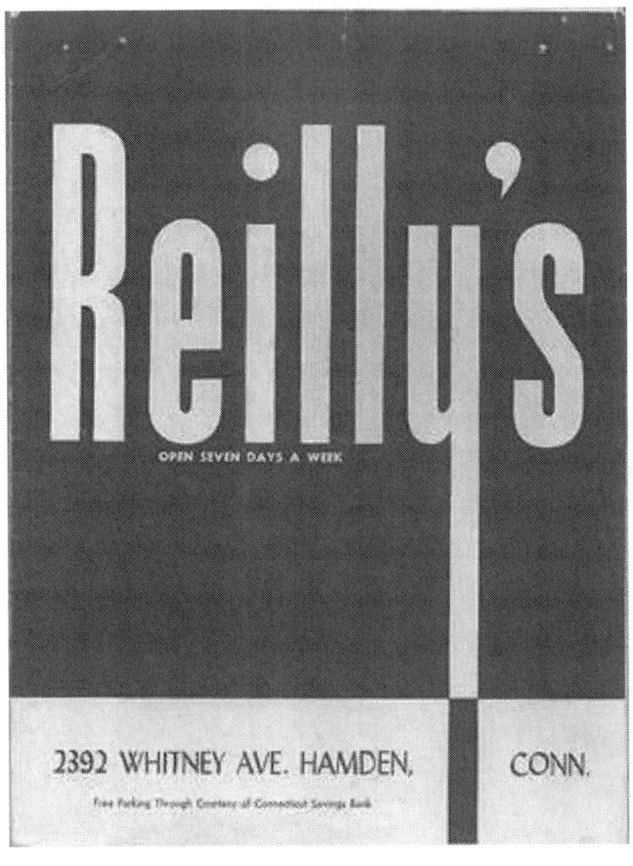

My boss Charlie Reilly had never been in the restaurant business before. George Harry set Charlie Reilly up in business. George was a Greek fellow. He had five restaurants in Yale. He set Charlie up in business in Hamden. I answered an ad that was looking for a chef. I went there and started working. Charlie had remodeled the restaurant, put everything in it , a big bar, everything. We had been there about a year and everything was going great. Then on Christmas Day, 1964, the whole place burned down. I was sitting in the house eating, had the radio on. A broadcaster from New York was on and he said a place in Hamden, a famous restaurant was on fire. He said the place is burning down, Reilly's Restaurant.

I said we just fixed that place up. I drove all the way from Cheshire, eight miles. The fire department was next door, right next door to the restaurant. Now it was Christmas morning and all the people from the fire department weren't there. Only one kid was there. When I got there the guy had a water hose at the back door. I had the key so I opened the door to the restaurant. I watched from across the street and something just blew up. The whole front, the windows and everything just busted out. The place just burnt down. I went in there afterward and took a dollar bill that had been up there and a few other things. I gave them to Charlie in a few weeks. He had to borrow money to rebuild the place, about sixty thousand dollars. They start building this new building that is still standing. It took them until November the next year to finish it. We opened up the new building on Thanksgiving. While they were building, I worked at another place. Some of our customers came there. They knew that when Reilly's was finished, I was going back. When we reopened our business was so good, we didn't have to advertise. In three months time, he made enough money to pay that loan back. I never saw the sun for three months. That's how much I worked. I worked and I worked and I worked. People used to come by and wonder how this man was so lucky to get someone like me. They wanted to know if I knew anybody who could do the things that I could do. Charlie was the same age as me and had five kids. This was the place everybody came to. All the big shots. He sold so much liquor. McDonald's came around and said they was going to put everybody out of business. I was selling my burgers for thirty cents. I think they was selling hamburgers for twenty cents. Well, I told the boss, this is what we are going to do. I'm going to make our hamburgers a little bigger, a quarter of a pound and I'm going to season them up. We're going to charge fifty cents a burger and that's what we did. For the first couple of days, people were going there and then they came back to me. I sold a lot of burgers. He bought a house on Ridge Road for 32 thousand dollars. At the time that was big money. Man, this guy made so much money, he sent his wife to Florida with her horse on a plane so she could ride it down there. Over the years our restaurant became famous. It was a good restaurant and at one point we had nine cooks. Charlie liked to drink a lot. My hours to work were from 5:30am to 1:30pm. Then I went home to rest and I would come back and work from 5pm to 9pm. The place was busy every day. One day I told my cooks that if one guy doesn't come in the other nine had to do the work. If two guys were out then the other eight had to do the work . If three were out then the other seven had to do the work. When it got down to if nobody doesn't show up but me, then I had to do all the work. Well, one day Charlie had been drinking and I wasn't there. When I came back he had fired everybody, so I had to do all the work. Every St. Patrick's Day we gave away free corn beef and cabbage. It was an exciting place to work. Along with Charlie some of the main people I met was was his brother George, his father Chester Reilly and his uncle David who was the bookkeeper. David looked like Dwight D Eisenhower, the president of the United States. He was a good man.

My boss used to advertise that we needed another chef. One day this guy, he was Irish, came in. He said he was a chef. He was talking to my boss. He was from Hartford, a big time chef. Then he came in the kitchen, talking to me. He came in and asked me my name. I said, Jeff. He said what time do you come in? I told him I usually come in very early to bake the rolls, stuff like that. He said well from now on, I'm the chef here. He said from now on you come in at nine or ten o'clock. He said he was going to come in early. Man, I started to trembling all over. I didn't know what to do. I ran out and saw the boss. I said boss, what did you do, fire me? He said, "what happened?" The guy was listening. Charlie said to him, " I told you to go in that kitchen and ask Jeff what time he wanted you to come in." Man, that guy got mad and run out. He said, "I don't want the job." This guy went away and came back in about two years. He asked me did I remember him. I said yeah, I think so. You was from Hartford, right. He said, let me tell you something. I'm sorry I didn't take the job here.

If I had, I would have learned something. He asked me did I need anybody now. I said yeah, I'll take you, anything you want to do. He worked with me for about six months. I had all kinds of people working for me there. Puerto Ricans, blacks, white. I had them all. Now the thing about Puerto Ricans was they worked together. If one Puerto Rican walked out, they all walked out. People got so they didn't want to hire Puerto Ricans. Well, I hired one and then I hired another. At one time I think I had about six Puerto Ricans working for me. They were hard working, honest people. I trained them. I trained one to be my second cook. I was at Reilly's nine or ten years. One night my boss got real drunk. I ran the kitchen, I made the menu. I bought what I wanted. I cooked what I wanted. He had nothing to say. I bought a thousand dollars worth of meat a week. We did so much business there. Anyway, that night I said something about something. I don't remember exactly what I said. He told me, he said, " This is my son. One day you'll be working for him." And I said to myself, why would he say that to me. I had the key and I walked out that night. I threw the key. It ended up in the soup pot. I just left. I didn't like what he said to me and I left. I worked there for about ten years.

Before I left Reilly's we decided to take a vacation. We went to Germany. My son Calvin, my daughter Dale, my wife and I. My wife's brother lived in Germany so we decided to go there. We stayed there three weeks. Before I went to Germany, I studied speaking German. Man, I could speak German. I studied for three months, records and all that. When we got there her brother and his wife had three kids. I used to do a lot of exercise like running. I was in top shape. I used to go out every morning. We used to have a short way getting to the town. I used to go the short way running and he would go the long way in the car. I used to beat him there. I used to run so fast. I used to walk the mountain. You could walk all the away around and never go in the road. I used to talk to those German people who used to walk. I could speak German. My brother-in-law, his name was Kirby. He was surprised that I could speak German. Sometimes we would go out to eat. It was cheap. Back in those days after World War II, our dollar was up there. Well, we left after three weeks. We got to the airport early in the morning. For twenty-two hours on the plane, I saw the sun. When we got to New York and got in the car, I still could see the sun. If I had went on to California, I still would have seen the sun for maybe 30 hours. When I came back the restaurant was a mess. I never took a vacation like that again.

I met this woman when I was working at Reilly's who said she was opening a restaurant at a place called Lake George. She said she needed a chef and asked me would I go there to work for her. She said she would pay me 150 per week. I said, "yes, I will go." This woman was married. Two weeks before we left for New York the woman's husband died. That did not stop us from going to Lake George. She had a fifteen-year-old son. He worked there for about two months. We served breakfast, lunch and dinner. Breakfast was the most important meal. The stove had twelve eyes so we could have twelve pans going at a time. We served mostly sausage, bacon and eggs. I remember one morning cooking thirty dozen eggs, fifteen pounds of bacon and fifteen pounds of sausage. I did that all by myself because my cook did not show up. I went to the boss and said when my help does not show up, I want his pay. I cannot remember what happened. I can remember I got another job on this ship named Ticonderoga. It left Lake George at 9am. It went up the lake to Vermont and returned at 4:30pm. I worked as a chef on that ship. The man hired me was from Florida. It was a summer job. He paid me 175 per week. The man who hired me had control over the food. The man who owned the ship took care of tourists, about 500 people. The man in charge of the food dismissed a chef who was a friend of the owner of the boat. The owner did not like that and so he gave me a hard time. He tried to make me quit, but my boss pleaded with me not to leave. The owner called me names, speaking recklessly to me. I stayed until the season was over. Here's the question. **Why do people treat me the way they do?**

Chapter 5

The Move To Cheshire, Ct.

While I was working at Reilly's, I moved to Cheshire Ct. I wanted to live in Cheshire mainly for one reason. I wanted my son Calvin to be able to go to a better school, I wanted him to go to go to Cheshire Academy.

He was smart and the schools in New Haven were lousy. We lived in Brookside in New Haven. Now some of the people in the neighborhood where I moved to, wanted to know who sold me the house in Cheshire. I bought this house from a guy teaching at Yale. He was from New Hampshire. I moved to Cheshire in the early sixties. The neighborhood was all white people. He felt black people had as much right to live out here as anybody else. Many of the people in the neighborhood put their house up for sale because black people moved in the area. I went out one night and the cops were blocking my driveway. They asked me what I was doing here. I told them I lived here. Most of the people out here were lawyers, things like that. My son always went out with white girls. This used to be all farmland with no trees and I used to be able to see all the way up the hill. The vice-president of Yale lived there and my son used to go out with his daughter. My son had a wreck in his car on 84 once and she was with him. The state trooper brought him home. While I was here the Ku Klux Klan burnt a cross on my lawn.

Cross burned on lawn

By BARBARA NECKER

CHESHIRE — A gasoline soaked wooden cross was burned Thursday night in the front yard of a black family that has lived peacefully in a south Cheshire neighborhood for 15 years.

Mrs. Otelia Evans of 49 Green Hill Lane said the burning was the third suspicious incident at her home in the last several days.

On Wednesday, she said, someone threw a flaming torch onto the hood of her 26-year-old son's car, scorching it slightly.

A few days before that, she said, her husband, Jeff, discovered a sizable rock on the roof, apparently thrown their deliberately.

Mrs. Evans also said the picture window of a white neighbor was recently smashed by a rock.

The three-to-four foot cross fired in front of the pink and white, attractive home left an X-shaped scorch mark on the Evans' lawn.

The Evans are one of three black families in the neighborhood, where houses range in value upward from $40,000. They experienced some harassment—such as garbage dumped on the lawn—when they first moved there from New Haven, but have since established friendly relations with most of their neighbors.

No one knows what triggered the event. Police believe the cross, wrapped in gasoline-soaked rags, was fired by youngsters, but Mrs. Evans wonders if it was really just a childish prank.

"It really sort of unnerved me last night," she said. "I just can't believe something like this."

Mrs. Evans said the flames were spotted about 10 p.m. by her husband, who was watching television at the time.

"At first I thought it was the house across the street," Evans said, pointing to a newly built, unoccupied house. "I wanted to get the hose."

Then he saw that it was a cross burning on his own lawn. He yelled to his wife, who was in the bedroom talking on the telephone.

Mrs. Evans called the police, then locked the back door and ran to the front door, where she and her husband watched the cross burn until it sputtered out.

Whoever did it, she said, is "sick. They [illegible] this not only to me."

She wondered why her family should be singled out. "We mind our own business, we work, we attend Bible class," she declared.

Her husband takes the incident philosophically.

"If a person has God in his heart—believing in Jesus Christ—then there is really nothing to worry about," he said.

Mrs. Evans said she and her family get on well with most of the neighbors, a statement that was verified by a young white neighbor girl.

The teenager, who did not want to be identified, said of the Evans', "They're fantastic. I really love them."

The cross-burning, she said, must have been "just a bunch of kids being stupid."

Mrs. Evans has been a nurse at Yale-New Haven Hospital since 1959, and her husband, a former chef and instructor at the Culinary Institute of America, is branching out into the restaurant consulting business. He hopes to build his own restaurant in Waterbury soon.

They threw garbage on my lawn. This is where I ask the question, **Why do people treat me the way they do?** I bought a 1954 mustang. The first mustang to come out. I went out one morning and they had scratched it from the front to the back. My son had a little car and they put stuff on it. One morning I went to vote and my neighbor was there. He said your place looks like hell. I had put elephant plants all around my house. There were also good white people living nearby who welcomed us to Cheshire. A family from down the street came up to us. There were six or seven children. They came up to us with a hearty welcome. I will never forget it. I also remember a little white girl named Jeannie Suprenant who would sit on my front door step. She was two or three at the time. Again the main reason I came to Cheshire was to give my son a chance for a great education. I moved here with my wife, my son who was twelve at the time, my daughter who was getting ready to go to college in Virginia and my daughter who had polio. We decided I would start cleaning up the place. It was a mess. The grass and bushes along with trees made it look like junk. I painted the house. I started cutting down trees and worked in the yard, cleaning it up. After I cleaned up the place, a lot of people came by. I had a beautiful lawn and they said you can teach us how to do things. I used to paint my house a different color every year and then in 1970, I decided to widen my driveway. I did it myself.

I had met the cops from Hamden. When I moved to Cheshire, Hamden only had two cops. I think Cheshire only had one or two. There were only two colored families living in Cheshire at that time. I think history, that means a lot. I just kept going and going. I been like this all my life. I don't hate anybody and people used to come by. They loved to talk to me and I loved to talk to them too, white people. But over the years seems like things would get better, but it seems like things have gotten worse.

Soon it was time to get my oldest girl Bunardy off to college. Also, I had to get my wife a car so she could go back and forth to work. She was a nurse at Yale Hospital in New Haven and we only had one car. I bought a new Volkswagen for my wife.

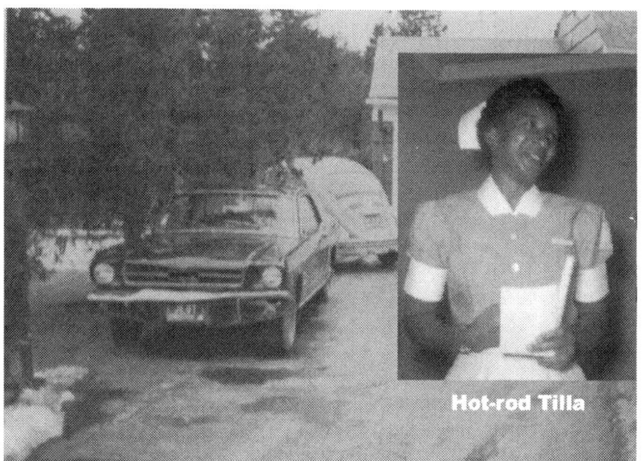
Hot-rod Tilla

It was a standard shift so I had to teach her in a hurry. I gave my wife driving lessons that day. The next day my wife and that Volkswagen went to work. She had a hard time driving and she called the car stupid. Sometimes when she stopped for a red light, she forgot to put the car in first gear, to start the car off. She had to learn to use her feet to mash the clutch to change the gears. She learned to use the clutch and the gears pretty fast, but after 10,000 miles she burned out the clutch. After that, she was on her way. You could drive that Volkswagen all week off of two dollars. She would be flying down the street and the street cop would wave for her to slow down. They started to call her hot-rod Tilla. After getting my wife on the road, I had to get myself on the road. I bought a bicycle. It cost $170.00 in 1960. It weighed nineteen pounds. I bought the Volkswagen and the bike because the Ford we had was burning too much gas. I needed to save on expenses to try to get ahead. I rode my bike to work every day and my wife drove her Volkswagen. I was happy riding my bike. My daughter was in college and my son was in Cheshire Academy. It was tough times, but I felt I was on my way and I thanked God for showing me the way. I rode my bicycle to work for three years, sometimes four times a day, winter and summer. Every day I entered the restaurant at 5:30 AM. My job was to bake 40 dozen dinner rolls and to get ready for lunch and dinner.

Let me talk about some people in my neighborhood which I have great respect for. Now some people say things before they think. A neighbor, I consider to be a friend in talking to me one day asked a question. He asked, "Why don't foreigners stay in their own neighborhood?" He was a foreigner. Why didn't he stay in his own neighborhood? You should not hate people for things they say, but you'll never get far over the years. Over the years, I seen a lot of things and I've done a lot of things. I remember painting my house every year for three years a different color. One side of my house, the west side needed paint every year. I decided to do something about it. I talked to my neighbor and asked him what could I do. He said to put vinyl siding on that side and you will never have to paint it again. I didn't know how to do it and he said he would show me. He told me what to buy. Along with siding over the years, I added a two car garage. I replaced the old garage and added twenty feet by twenty-four feet on that side. It was like another house. You could enter the kitchen now through the garage. It had a full bath and a fireplace. It had an upstairs and a downstairs. Now I knew if I put vinyl siding on that side of the house it would look good. I wanted to know how much it would cost to put siding on the whole house. I talked to several contractors who did that kind of work. The estimates the estimates were from $15,000-$18,000. After all that I had to make up my mind. After talking to my neighbor Jack, I decided to do it myself. I started to work in September 1979. I remember reading in the newspaper that for people insulating their house, the government would give a tax break. You could save a lot of money over the years. I figured it would cost me 3,000 for the whole house. I started to work by first putting black bond over the top of the shingles. Then I put vinyl siding on top of the black bond. Then I nailed it all together. During the time of working on the house, I was working as top chef in a restaurant in Durham. I worked at night from 4pm to 11pm. I got home at 12am, I went to bed and got up at 7am to work on the house. I said to myself, I will finish by Christmas. I completed the job December 15th, 1979. I did it all by myself. I left the job in Durham in 1980. A friend of my daughter's husband wanted me to take over the food department in North Haven. He would take care of the liquor and I would take over the food department. I was there awhile, business started to get good. I started to make money. Then he wanted me to pay rent. He wanted part of the money I was making. I called my wife's brother who was in Germany. He came and wanted to be my partner. He worked awhile but too much money was going out. He quit and went back to Germany. I said I would quit also. I pulled my Volkswagen up to the back door. I put my portable salad bar, pots and pans in my Volkswagen and left.

Chapter 6
Teaching The Trade

When the culinary school first opened in New Haven, I was the first one in line. I wanted to be a chef. I remember in Washington D.C., I used to look at what those guys were doing at work and I liked it. I wanted to be a chef. I knew how to work on a farm. I knew how to pick cotton. Things like that I could do. But being a chef was something I didn't know anything about. The Culinary Institute Of America started on State Street. They first called it the New Haven Restaurant Institute. We graduated at the Taft hotel. Mrs. Angell donated the school. Her husband was the president of Yale. Even while I was going to school, I used to go up to her house. She lived in Hamden, off Whitney Avenue. I used to rake the leaves and stuff like that. She was one of the most beautiful ladies I ever saw. She was really nice. We started on State Street in a big storefront. We had about fifteen students at first. A lot of people in the school had already been out in the field cooking. They came back to learn extra things, like cooking pastry, things like that. Well the CIA gave me my start.

I got my first job really teaching in Stamford. The government wanted people to train in the ghetto. So I got a job in Stamford. I used to go into the unemployment office and grab candidates who wanted to cook. I got all my customers from the unemployment office. They used to send them to me. I used to train them at night in the high school. We got along good. I used to buy the food and teach them the things they needed to know about cooking. Then once they graduated, I would take them to restaurants and help them, showing them how to do things. It was a good set up. Then the guy called me from the Culinary Institute. They needed a black guy. So I start teaching in New Haven. Then they moved the school to New York. It was a soft job, six hours a day. It was only $200 a week. I was happy to get it. I was living up in the dormitory in Hyde Park. We had over 1,000 students there. But when I was in New Haven they had this guy from Bridgeport. He hated black people. He told Mr. Roth I didn't do my job. He said I kept a dirty kitchen. Well, some students said they would help me and when we went to New York, they cleaned that kitchen spotless. Well, I became kind of famous there. I used to be able to take the bones out of chicken and turkey without cutting the skin. I did that for my wife one time at Christmas and she cried like a baby. She came home from work and saw that turkey laying flat and said what did you do to my turkey. I said all you have to do is put stuffing in it. I start putting stuffing in in the wings, stuffing in the legs. Then she started smiling. She said now it looks like a turkey. I got criticized at Hyde Park. They said I did not know how to teach. We had a guy from France. He was a top chef. The owner decided he would try something. He said I'm going to give the students a chance to criticize the teachers. I am going to let each teacher talk about five minutes. We got training from teachers to teach us how to teach. Just like people like mayors get help to run things, we were getting help to teach. We had about 100 teachers there. I used to bone the chicken in front of the class. Well, it was my time to talk and everybody started laughing. After I finished the guy in charge asked, "Mr. Evans how long have you been teaching?" I said, "I have three kids and I've been teaching them ever since they were young. I've been teaching them how to do things and how to live. He said the way you are teaching here is the same way I teach. He said you are teaching the way we tell you to teach. You are right up-to-date. The next morning I went up to the head of the school. I knocked on the door and no one said to come in so I just pushed the door open. The lady hollered what do you want. I said I have to see Mr. Roth. I have something to tell him. She said you can't go in there. I just kept walking. I pushed the door open. He said what do you want. I said Mr. Roth you know the man that you hired from Connecticut to teach us how to teach? I would like you to call him up and ask him what type of teacher I am. He talked to that man that day, he called him up. So that night after class I went to get my mail to see what I have to do the next day. The guy under Mr. Roth had a letter in there. The letter said thank you for your superior teaching. It went all over the school,

Mr. Evans is a great teacher. Students were saying I'll be glad to get into your class. I heard you are teaching good things. I made history. I stayed there for some years. I got letters from the students' mothers praising me, saying I was a great teacher to their children. I tried to teach the students about cooking and life.

Profile

Jefferson Evans

Chef/Instructor, The Culinary Institute, Class of 1948

This article is a condensed version of one written by junior Ralph Reissman in La Toque Blanche, the C.I.A.'s student paper.

Jefferson Evans, Chef/Instructor at The Culinary Institute of America is a graduate of the first class ever established by school twenty-six years ago. In 1946, Evans and ten other students studied and cooked in a downtown New Haven storefront, preparing only one meal with one main course daily, as opposed to today's practice of producing four and five entrees twice a day.

Today, the food service industry is searching for qualified workers, but how did chef Evans make his way "in the field" after receiving his diploma? He recounts that he went to a restaurant looking for a job, whereupon the owner and chef took him right to the kitchen. "He told me to make him a brown sauce. So I made a mirepoix, made the roux and added a little brown stock, just like I learned in school. Then he told me to me to bone a ham, and I did that too. Then he says, after he looks me up and down once or twice, 'I don't know how much to pay you. You are too good!'"

Chef Evans holds a philosophy of life that has carried him through the most difficult times and helped him to achieve his goals. He holds that people fall into two categories: "the one hundred per-centers and the fifty per-centers." The essence of the philosophy is his favorite aphorism, one he coined himself: "It's not as hard as you think to be best."

"If I'm not going to give it all I've got, I might as well stay in bed," says Evans. "What good am I going to do me, my job, or my boss?" he notes. "You can't let a fifty percenter pull you down to his level. You have to make up for him just to get the job done right, so it means doing your job and his while he just wastes his time. What good would it do me to do a half-way job, and be a fifty percenter? If you do your best, and you know you are doing your best, things just have to get better."

This attitude can be demonstrated by Chef Evan's experience even while not in the cooking field. About twenty years ago, he simply could not get a job as a chef so he turned to house painting. Assigned by a contractor to paint a whole development along with another worker, Evans was set back when this fellow did nothing for the week except to sit on the bottom rung of the ladder while Evans painted. Not wanting to lose this job in any event, Evans did the job for both, working twice as hard and making no comments either to the worker or the boss. When Monday came, the contractor fired the other worker and invited Evans to stay on his own. Actually the contractor had been aware of the whole situation.

When he found an opening in the culinary field Chef Evans worked eighteen hours a day, seven days a week for seven months until Reilly's, a restaurant in Connecticut was making money. When he left after twenty years, Reilly's was grossing ten thousand dollars per week.

Chef Evans' philosophy is in full operation at the C.I.A. too. He runs, never walks anywhere in or out of the kitchen. A familiar cry of "Chef" punctuates the busy harmony of the kitchen, and Chef Evans can be seen darting around the corners trying to keep up with the requests for help, advice, or just a plain "Right on, right on". On the blackboard over the menu was written: "Hi Chef. Right on, right on, right on."

When the nightly meal is over, Chef Evans is immediately preparing for the following day, checking stores and planning assignments. On weekends, though he almost always relaxes at home in Connecticut with his wife, a working registered nurse. His children are all adults. "The first thing I do when I get home is to go right to the refrigerator, so that I can see what she has been eating." He cannot sit still for too long, though, and exercises every morning, jogs regularly, and looks not a day over thirty-five, although he is at least ten years older. His eyes radiant with sparkling energy and deep with experience and understanding, are set in a permanently furrowed brow, brought on from constant thought and effort, the effort of a one hundred percenter.

Chef Evans is impressed by the earnestness and effort of today's student body. Basic theoritical knowledge will serve as a unifying force when out in the field, he says, but there is no avoiding the hard work and experience to make one polished Chef de Cuisine. Until they reach that point, C.I.A. students can profit from the knowledge and understanding of one of the first students to prove our school's worth: Chef Jefferson Evans.

8

This article was written when I taught at the CIA at Hyde Park, New York.

Then I got a job in Branford during the summer. The guy said I'll give you the job, but you see that white guy over there. You have to be twice as good as him. I said I could do it. He gave me the job and I worked there for a couple of summers. One year in October, the school was about to start. The students came up to me saying, Mr. Evans, we're so glad we got you. Will you teach us the same things that you've been teaching the other students? I told them well since I've been here today, I've been through this program and they told me to teach them the basics. Teach them how to light the stove. Teach them how to put water in the pot. Teach them how to keep the place clean. Just teach them what's in the book, the curriculum and nothing more. Things that I like to teach about, let's say leftover food, I can't teach you that. They said Mr. Evans would you get in trouble if we go upstairs and talk to the main guy about it. I said no. I'm already in trouble. I've been in trouble all my life with people telling me I don't know how to do things. I said no, you make me feel good if you do that. Well, they went up there and they told the coordinator guy they wanted me to teach them the things that I taught their friends. The president, the guy in charge heard about it and he thought it was a great idea. The coordinators cussed me out saying that I sent the kids up there to hurt them. I told them, I didn't send them up there. Well, they didn't believe it. The next day I went up there and told them I was resigning from the school. Well, this got all over the school. Some of the kids wanted to go on a strike. I called a meeting. I told them that you're here now. Make the best of it. Don't give up. Somebody here will teach you a lot of things. So I left. I called this guy and I went up to Johnson and Wales. I had all my tools and I left. My box that I had my tools in, it didn't look too good. It was rusty. The coordinator there got on me about that. I didn't really think that was nice of him but I painted it and I made it look good. Two weeks later after he fussed me out, he died. It seems like during my lifetime people who give me a hard time, people who didn't like me, sooner or later they die.

I stayed at Johnson and Wales and taught there a few years. A few years ago, Johnson and Wales and the Culinary Institute of America along with The Black Culinarian Alliance, gave me an honor. At Hyde Park, there is an award called the Jefferson Evans Award. They started the award in 1995. It was started by the Black Culinarian Alliance(BCA). The man who started the BCA and the main guy to give me the award is named Alex Askew. He is a great man.

Alex Askew

This is one of the articles that was in a newspaper.

Industry to honor

Jefferson Evans

PROVIDENCE R.I. On Feb. 11, the national leaders in culinary and foodservice education – Johnson & Wales University and the Culinary Institute of America – will partner with the Black Culinary Alliance's first student chapter to honor Jefferson Evans, the first black graduate of the CIA, class of 1947.

Johnson & Wales will host the event here on its main campus in its new culinary lab, The Center for Culinary Excellence. There will be a reception, tributes to Jefferson and a three-course meal prepared by students of both schools. Officials of J&W and the CIA expressed pride about their first-ever collaboration to celebrate diversity by honoring a distinguished alumnus.

"This is a historic event for both colleges because, though we and the CIA are competitors, we both believe in excellence in culinary education and share the highest reputation in the world for the same," said Karl Guggenmos, dean of culinary education at Johnson & Wales. "We are especially committed to supporting diversity within our industry."

Eve Felder, associate dean for culinary arts at CIA, emphasizes Evans' long-standing contributions to the field: "The Culinary Institute of America is honored to join in this celebration of the accomplishments of Jefferson Evans. As both an alumnus of the CIA and a past member of our faculty, chef Evans has a distinguished legacy in culinary education that truly expresses our college values of excellence and respect for diversity."

There were some other papers who did articles on me like in my town, The Cheshire Herald did a story on me.

Cooking Up Memories: Jefferson Evans A Pioneer For Minority Chefs

THE CHESHIRE HERALD, MARCH 25, 2004

Entertainment...

Cheshire Chef Shares His Talents Through Teaching

The people from Johnson and Wales came and did a six minute film on me. The name of It was, “A Few Episodes In The Life of Jefferson Evans.” (link) https://youtu.be/2xVQg9MsjBo

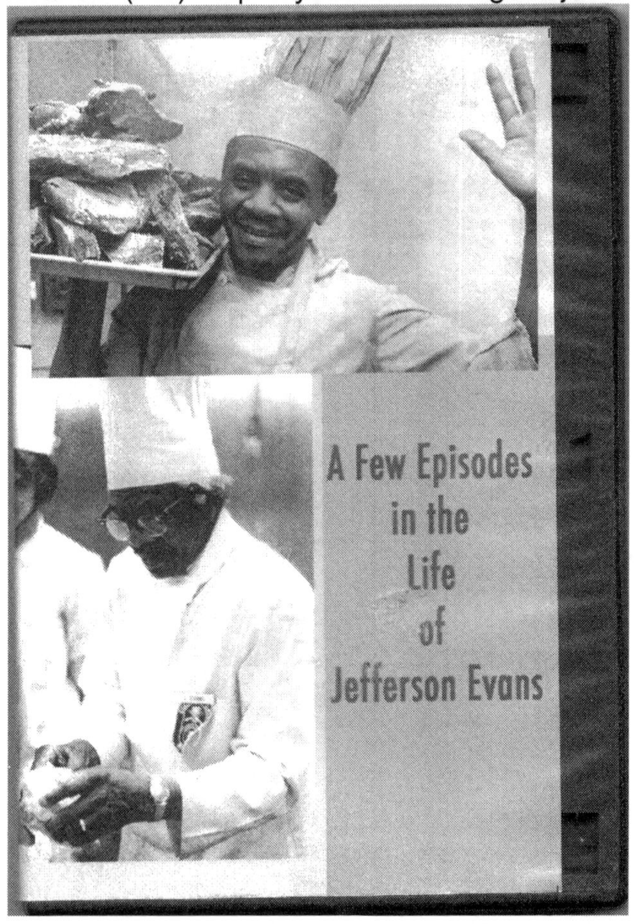

A young lady named Hilary came to my house.

She is an artist. She took pictures of me to use in her art. They came out great. She even used those pictures in her art show.

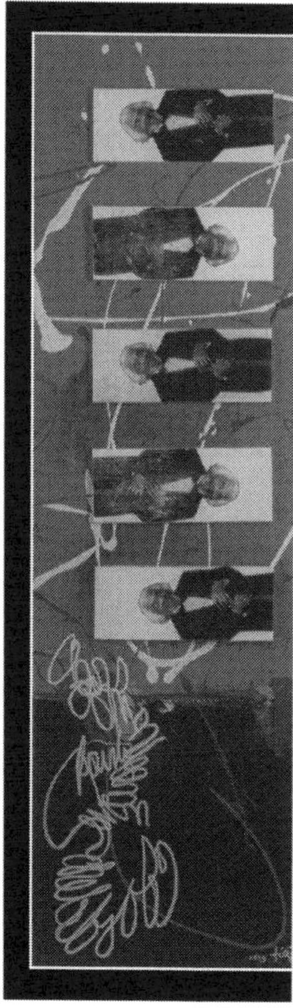

She wrote a paper about it too.

"HONORARY ABSTRACTS"

Chef Jefferson Evans (first in a series)

Hilary Blackman

The New Century Artists Gallery

February 19, 2013 – March 2, 2013

While exhibiting at the New York Times in January 2012 I was approached by Alex Askew the President of the Black Culinary Alliance to consider work on a series about African-American Chefs and their contributions to the hospitality and Culinary Industry. I was immediately excited about the opportunity to meet surviving culinary greats, to hear their stories and to produce a body of work that could honor and celebrate their legacy.

I began work in May 2012 by visiting our first, Chef Jefferson Evans (89yrs old). We went to his home in Cheshire, Connecticut where he currently resides. Chef Jefferson Evans was the first African American to graduate from the Culinary Institute of America in 1947. What a special opportunity this was.

I made the trek to his home with a camera crew of two in order to capture the meeting and to record his words. It was an early afternoon with not a cloud in the sky, air was crisp and the sun seemed to be shining a little extra on this particular house on the corner. It was that of Chef Jeff.

We rang the bell and when Chef Jeff opened the door he had a presence that was gentle but great indeed. I saw a beautiful caramel complexion face, his eyes were innocent yet very deliberately focused, hidden behind a pair of wire rim glasses that set gently on his nose. His face was framed by a beautiful head of silver gray hair that flowed to the top of his shoulders much like that of Fredrick Douglas. He wore a plaid shirt and black dress pants. His walk was somewhat slanted due to arthritis in his knees that he later explained came from hours of standing in the kitchen throughout his career. When we arrived he graciously let us in and asked us to have a seat as he served lunch to his 93-year wife. He had prepared fresh carrot juice with all sorts of spices; he fixed a baked chicken, potatoes and string beans. The way he cared for her so lovingly was really special to watch.

When we started to interview and tape, Chef Jeff came alive with excitement. He spoke of his childhood days back in Crawfordville, Georgia. He shared stories about the years he taught at Johnson and Wales, the many struggles and challenges he faced in the field, the restaurant he owned called "the One and Only", and we learned that he survived the death of two of his three children.

To have been in his presence for that one afternoon left an indelible impression on my heart. My appreciation for His trials and the triumphs reached a high that day and inspired a fire within me. I started sketches not too long after that, to produce a body of art for him that would capture his essence and the strength of his hidden legacy. I now term the works that will be produced as a part of this collection as "Honorary Abstracts".

Concepts Revisited...

As an artist you must remain true to the process as your work develops in different directions. With Art that I previously produced I wanted to capture and display the most basic principles such as perspective, dimension and color completing works that were more literal. Most recently, I am committed to each piece capturing an energy that is derived from an abstract interpretation while still utilizing the same skills and principles. The abstract interpretation almost always forces a viewer to participate, taking them back to their own mind and what is coming up for them. This is important because while my intent is important, the individual experience that my viewers will have is just as vital. The abstract adds an element of imagination for the viewer that is not always the obvious. So I invite you to look at each piece and think about the emotions or energy that come up for you about who Jefferson Evans was and is and always will be as he will forever exist in our history.

Hilary Blackman
Visual Artist

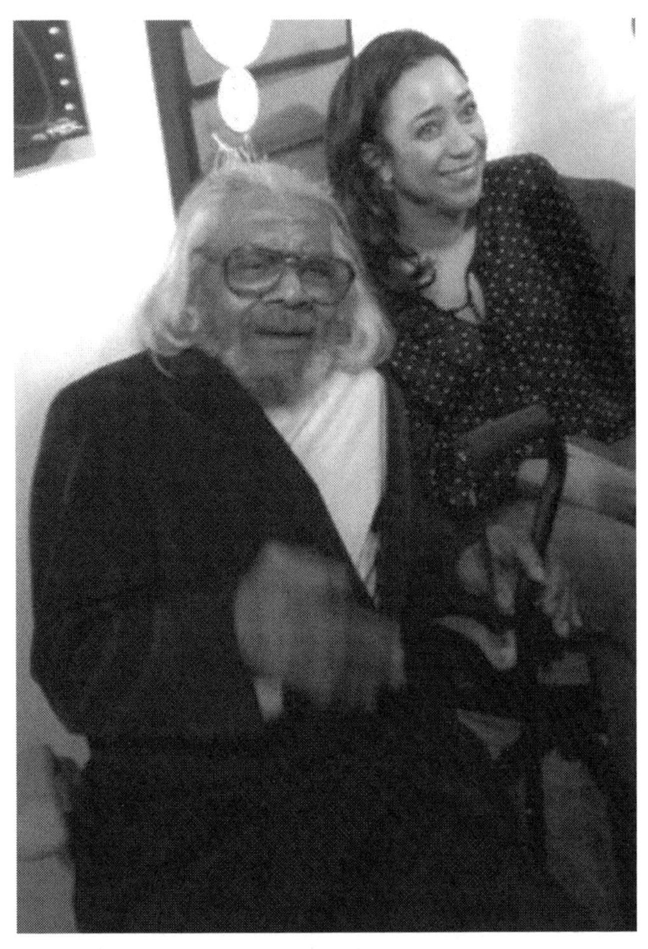

Hilary and I

The City of White Plains took a day to honor me. A lot of people were there that day.

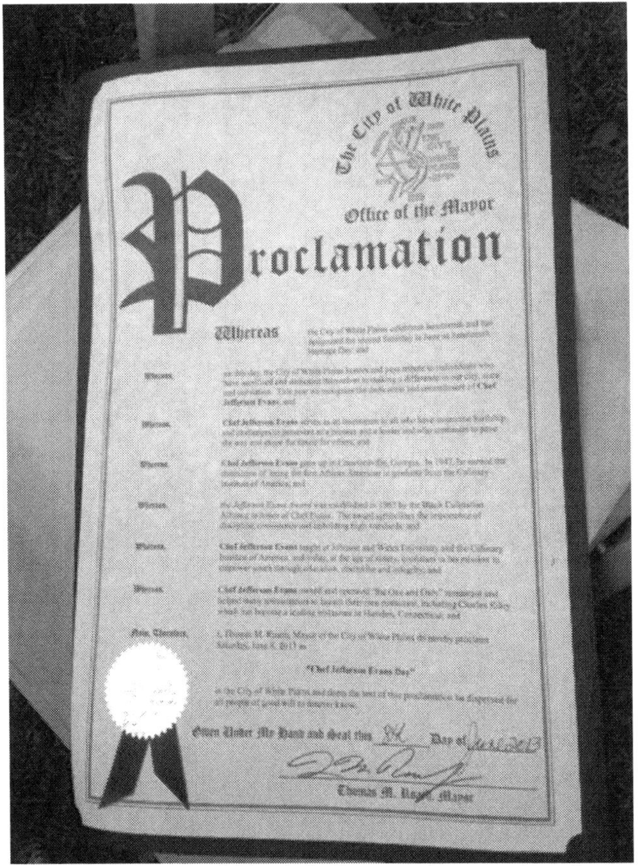
The City of White Plains

Office of the Mayor

Proclamation

Whereas

They called it, "Chef Jefferson Evans Day"

Even the mayor was there. It was a lot of fun.

Chapter 7

The One 'N' Only Restaurant

Lunch
Menu
One 'N' Only
Restaurant
New Haven, Connecticut

I opened up a restaurant on Dixwell Avenue. The building was owned by my daughter's husband Brack. I gave him $10,000 to make over the building and I didn't have to pay rent for the first year. After the first year, I think I had to pay seven hundred dollars a month. Then I started to look for supplies. I went all over the state. In a small town, Stafford Connecticut, I found a restaurant that just went out of business. I purchased the total supplies for $10,000. After a few months, the building had a new look. Brack and his Six Carpenters fixed it up and after they fixed it up, I moved in. It was hard because in starting a restaurant you had to buy everything. We had to apply for a restaurant license and then wait for inspection. After we got the okay to open, I started to order food. I went down to Standard Beef. Hank, the guy who owned it was my friend. His father had owned it. When I first met Hank, Hank was a little boy. I had given his father a lot of business over the years. So I needed help and I went to him and ordered a thousand dollars worth of food. He sent that food and didn't ask any questions. That week, I made enough money to pay him and never asked him for credit again in the seven or eight years I was in business. I started hiring people to work, waitresses, cooks and dishwashers. In hiring people you have to be fair. I said to myself, I'll be good to him and he will stay with me a long time. I found that to be not true. My ideal thought was to be fair and work the hell out of him.

The name of my restaurant was, "The One 'N' Only." My wife named it. The first day we opened was good. My idea was to open a gourmet restaurant. I stayed with that idea for two days. I had to change the menu to chitlins, pork chops, meatloaf, hot dogs, pig feet, collard greens, hamburgers. In other words soul food. In order to do good in the restaurant business, you have to hire and fire people. The people you hire should have a little training or you can train them. I trained a lot of people having been in the business for almost 60 years. Some people acted like they knew more than me. They were telling me how to do things. In six months, I went through about 70 people. Some just wouldn't listen. When I opened the restaurant my wife was working at Yale. She took three months off to help me. She really enjoyed working in the restaurant. She worked at the cash register she watched everything.

Then something went wrong. The people I would tell what to do would run to my wife. They wanted my wife to fire me. After a while, she felt it was too hard. After she went back to work, she would bring me donuts. I would put them on the menu. Dealing with people is not easy. You have to be good and hard. Before I sold the restaurant, my mother came here from

Georgia. She brought my aunt with her. She stayed with me a whole week. Oh, she was really proud of me. She was so happy to see me. I had this big restaurant, I was doing pretty good. I had a house that was paid for. My wife was a nurse working at the hospital.

I got at the restaurant very early, at five in the morning. I would bake rolls. I opened up at 5:30. People were there to eat breakfast. I started off with waitresses and cooks. So many people came in and said they were a waitress. I must have changed in a month at least ten waitresses. They come there and after two days they wanted to tell me what to do. I had a breakfast menu. The cheapest item was 95 cents. As life went on I had a big breakfast menu, a lunch and a dinner menu. I never really made much money. I had seven, eight, up to ten people working for me. They stole from me. I had to watch them. But I stayed there four or five years and then I just got tired and closed up. At some point, Brack had sold the building to this white guy. I had been paying $700 a month for rent. The next month he raised my rent to $1,200 a month. The final straw was when I got insurance from this black guy. I gave him the money and he didn't even put the money in. The Hartford Insurance Company sent me a letter. I had paid him seven or eight hundred dollars and they sent me a letter saying they were going to cancel my insurance. I asked him did he pay the insurance and he said give me some more money and he could straighten it out. Oh God, I said to myself, I ain't giving you no money. That day I decided I was going to close. I didn't tell anybody. That day this lady was walking down the aisle in my restaurant and she almost stumbled. I know I didn't have any insurance. I said Lord, please don't fall. That night I walked out of that restaurant. I closed it up and never went back. I took all my stuff out and sold it to different people. I started working construction with Brack and doing other jobs with people. From then on, I said the best thing for me to do is to get out of the restaurant business and that's what I did. I have to ask the question.

Why do people treat me the way they do?

The newspaper had an article about me. That's when I started working for

City restaurateur retiring while he's still 'young'

the government. The government was giving out a lot of money. That's when Johnson was president. They were giving money for all types of programs, people going to school, photography school, beauty school, hairdressing school. A lot of small business opened up. I was working for this organization as a chef teaching. I worked in Stamford at night. I would recruit from the unemployment office and get these guys to teach them how to cook. They gave you money to buy food to teach the guys. You would buy so much food for the class. I had a lot of money left over. My boss said you should have spent it. I gave it back to the government. It was only one meal you cooked at night. I took the guys to different restaurants after I trained them. I would find jobs for them. At first, they worked for free. I would stay with them at the restaurant for an hour or so, so they could understand what they were doing. Some of the students used to drink. I had one student with me and I had 20 dollars in the glove compartment and he stole it. After that, I got tired and quit.

Then I got a chance to go to a school in Cheshire. It was a elementary school for the little kids. They saw my picture in the paper and invited me there. I went with my wife. Those kids wanted to help me do my book, but my wife and daughter did not think it was a good idea.

Jefferson Evans, right, and his wife, Otelia, at their Cheshire home. Evans, who had a long career in restaurants, will lead a coo[king] class this month and next.

A pioneer of cooking

Cheshire resident Jefferson Evans was the first black graduate of the Culinary Institute of America in 1947

By Ralph Hohman
Record-Journal staff

Jefferson Evans has packed a lot of history into eight decades. He's trying to get it all down on paper, writing an autobiography, longhand.

"It's pretty hard, you know, when you get to be my age and try to write," Evans says amid the knickknacks and family pictures in his cozy living room. He's wearing a blue, red and mostly light-gray warm-up suit. His coarse, silver-white hair is pulled back into a ponytail that his wife, Otelia Evans, doesn't much care for.

"You forget how to spell and your mind runs in different ways," he continues. "You're not like you used to be."

Evans says his next birthday will be 81 (though he also says he's OK with records that say he's 82). A Cheshire resident since 1962 and now mostly retired, he still owns and manages a rental property in New Haven. According to Otelia, he can still do yard work with a vengeance.

Jefferson Evans's brush with fame, though, comes from being a pioneer.

He'd intended to go to Yale after finishing his Army service during World War II — a stint he says was all stateside because of gunshot wounds to both knees that he got from an associate who owed him money and tried to settle up with a gun. It will all be in the book, Evans says.

His mother had been a teacher who had gone to Spelman College in Atlanta, he says. She stressed reading and learning, although the message didn't always get through. Evans' life was rich in other ways.

"My grandfather, he was like a big shot," he says. "Everybody in the South wasn't poor — he had 430 acres of land, my grandfather did."

Evans says he learned how to work hard on that big farm in Georgia.

"My mother used to have a baby this morning, and she was out in the field that afternoon," he says. "We had 12 kids, and it was just one of those things. People were strong."

It's something he carried with him through construction and truck-driving jobs in Washington, D.C., and all the other things he did after coming to Connecticut.

Getting an Ivy League education wasn't one of them.

"I had some nerve to say I [illegible] going to Yale," he says.

But the New Haven Resta[urant] Institute was just opening up, [and] the GI Bill would pay for Eva[ns to] attend that, too. He gained ac[cep]tance to what has long since [ex]panded, moved to Hyde Park, [N.Y.,] and changed its name to the [Culi]nary Institute of America.

The school, which says it ha[s an] enrollment of 400 students, [ac]knowledges that Evans was its [first] black graduate, part of the cla[ss of] '47. And while racism limited [his] employment prospects in the 1[940s] and beyond, Evans says he al[so] made himself independ[ent] through a series of restaurant [jobs] by networking his competition.

Please see Cooking

Chapter 8

The Family-
Brothers and
Sisters

Let me tell you about my wife's family. My wife was born in Virginia. Her mother died when she was ten years old. Her father got married again. My wife moved to Philadelphia, Pennsylvania to live with her people. My wife had one sister. When my wife moved to Philadelphia her sister stayed with her father and his new wife. My wife had four brothers. They also went to Philadelphia. When World War II started, my wife and her brothers moved to New Haven, Ct. My wife's brothers were named Ray, Neil and Pete. I don't remember the name of the fourth one. He died young. Her sister's name was Jean. During the war, Neil and Pete went into the army. My wife's brothers were very smart. They were upholsterers. Neil built televisions. My wife's sister Jean also came to Connecticut. She was eighteen when I met her. She lived with us for a while. She was rough and tough. She could hold me down. She was rugged. Ray made clothes. He had a church in North Haven, Ct. Ray had a daughter named Bush and a son named Ray. Bush's real name was Valerie. She lives in New York and her family is beautiful. The son, Ray went into the army. He died at a young age. The daughter Bush moved to New York. Ray and Pete both died at the age of fifty. Pete had five children. They lived in West Haven, Ct. He built his own house. He had one son and four girls. His wife still lives in the house that he built.

Pete's son, Arnold became a minister. The girls are named Theresa, Thomasine and Joyce. I don't remember the other girl's name. Pete's wife was named Dorothy. Theresa was a minister also. She lives in New York and her family is beautiful. After the war, Neil decided he could not make it in the USA. He decided he would go to Germany. He got married to a German woman.

He had two boys and two girls. One girl died when she was 14 years old. One boy lives in Maine. The other boy still lives in Germany along with his wife. They used to visit us ever year.

Let me tell you about my family. My oldest brother is named Virtus. My second sister was named Ann. She had two kids. She has one boy and one girl. The boy died early in life but the girl is still living, old enough to retire by now. I am the third child, Jeff. The fourth child was my sister Mattie. She lived in Maryland. She lived in a beautiful house. She had one child, a boy who died early. She was one of my favorite sisters. The fifth child was Barbara. She lived in Atlanta, Georgia. Barbara had one girl who lives in Atlanta and is a school teacher. Her name is Joyce. Joyce lived with my mother and father from a baby until she was grown up. She went to college and then she got married, but she has no children. My sister Barbara lived with her in Atlanta where Joyce is a teacher. My mother is a teacher. I am a teacher(smile). My sister Ella, the sixth child lived in New Jersey. She had three girls. Roberta teaches about computers, Debra stars in movies and Salina is a social worker in New Jersey. The seventh child, my sister Doris had four boys. One son is a minister named Stanley Dixon. His wife is from England. He has four boys. They visited me one September. Doris' oldest son is named Larry Dixon. He has one child and his wife is named Vivian. She is a teacher. His daughter went to college. The eighth child is named Alvin. He is a twin. He has a good trade. He builds houses and something else. He is married. and he has two girls. One is named Jackie. They both went to college. The ninth child, his twin brother Calvin, died five months after he was born. The tenth child was my sister Iristeen. She was a beautiful little girl. She died at age eight. The eleventh child was my brother John. He died in 1990. He had three boys and two girls. He was a cabinet maker. He did good work. The boys took over the business. They all finished college. The twelfth child is my sister who we call Treat. Her name is Melba. She had five boys. They live in Atlanta. Before my mother died she gave us all a piece of land in Georgia. The last child was my brother Burbank. He was born in 1941. He was my mother's baby. At that time my mother's sister was living with us. She babied him. He was a momma's baby. My mother's sister name was Sarah. She was crippled. I had an older brother and an older sister who died at birth. I can't talk about them. I can tell you a little about my oldest brother Virtus. He was in Connecticut at my surprise birthday party when I turned eighty. As a matter of fact, My sisters Barbara, Ella and Mattie and my brother Alvin were at the party too.

My sisters, Barbara and Ella

My wife, my sister Mattie, myself and others looking on at my eightieth birthday party.

My brothers Virtus and Alvin and me.

My daughter Buni surprised me with an 80th birthday party. This is me, Buni and my wife.

Even some of the neighbors were there.

Virtus came out of the army after World War II, got married, went to D.C. and went to school. His wife, Indiana went to school and became a number one teacher.

Indiana Stewart Evans Selected By Radio Station 102.3 & Aunt Jemima As Mother Of The Year

Mrs. Indiana Stewart Evans, who is a former resident of Crawfordville, has been selected by Magic Radio Station 102.3 and Aunt Jemima to be the Mother of the Year for 2007.

I was married to the late Mr. Virtus E. Evans for 58 years. I am the daughter of the late Deacon Lonnie Stewart and Mrs. Mary Stewart. Growing up on a farm there with my parents and seven siblings has left many fond memories of my childhood. Friendship Baptist Church became my home church at the age of 11. My early education started at Winbern Elementary School in a one-room school. Then I attended Winbern Jr. High. I graduated from Murden High School, Crawfordville, as the Valedictorian of my class. Georgia State College in Savannah became my first college. I also taught school in Crawfordville at Roanoke and Level Hill Elementary Schools.

After I got married we moved to Washington, DC. I attended Howard University and D.C. Teachers College. I graduated from D.C. Teacher's College and attended Trinity University Graduate School. Having taught elementary school in D.C. for thirty-four years, I retired, but I was not ready to leave the children, and I taught at Job Corps for another 5 years. I felt like I was a mother to every child whose life I touched because I truly loved them all.

I am the mother of six. One is deceased. My husband and I felt like it was our responsibility to make sure each child reached his potential; and we were blessed that every child attended college. Four of them have master's degrees, and one has a Ph.D. I have eight grandchildren, and four have graduated from college, and two are still in college. One will complete her master's degree in May. One has her MEA from Columbia University in New York. One grandson just completed his second year of Medical School at Virginia Commonwealth University in Richmond. Two are still in elementary school.

I am so proud of my family's success, and I know that God is just blessing us, and I know that our parental involvement, our great love, our patience, our understanding, and our endurance also helped to make them successful. We were never too busy to listen to their problems and help them find solutions. We also attended Sunday School and church together. We also prayed together. We tried hard to avoid criticism. We would always praise them and dwell on positive things, and God truly blessed us. And He is still pouring His blessing upon us.

I attend Bibleway Temple and work as a circle leader. As Mother of the Year, I saw the play, "Love in the Nick of Time". I met Morris Chestnut and the entire cast backstage. My additional prizes include maid service once a month, spa services once a month, and fresh flowers once a month. All of these prizes will be for the whole year.

I am so elated over being chosen Mother of the Year! It is truly a blessing from God. I am so thankful that Crawfordville gave me my religious and educational background so that I could be successful in life.

(Editor's Note: What a wonderful success story! Your hometown community is proud to hear from you. Congratulations and thanks for sharing!)

They had five children together. The oldest girl went to school. She became a doctor. The oldest son died. The second son is named Anthony. He teaches electronics and computers. Police killed his other son in the back yard of their house. Their second daughter is named Yvonne. She is a teacher in North Carolina. She has one child. I also want to say a little about my brother Burbank. He is the one with ten children. He took care of the home establishment. He was an auto mechanic, working on automobiles. Now when I was about ten years old, I was the weatherman. I would tell my father when it going to rain, sometimes two weeks before it would rain. It would rain the day I said. So everybody called me the weatherman.

Chapter 9

My Daughters And My Son

Dale was born in 1948. She was born with polio. She only weighed about two or three pounds. She was born at St Raphael's Hospital. She stayed in the hospital for her first six months. She didn't start walking until she was three to four years old. She was a nice girl. When she started to school, she was kind of slow, but she was a beautiful girl. She went to school in Brookside. She also had tutors to work with her. She loved to eat. She loved me, her daddy. When she was young, I used to carry her around. She was such a sweet girl. When my mother saw her she said she was just like her sister Lil. Her sister Lil was crippled too. Dale ran away from home once. She must have been about ten or eleven years old. She was over in Wallingford. Dale was a great talker. She loved to talk. She loved to be with people. She would meet you and it would be like she knew you all your life. She used to go to Sunday school every week. A lady name Ms. Tyson used to pick her up. One day when she came from Sunday school, I hid behind the door. She had her own key to come in. She went right to the refrigerator and started eating and eating. I looked at her and said Dale, you know you not supposed to be eating what you eating. When she grew up she worked a little with special jobs that she had. She used to work at a school and one day met Mayor Richard Lee who was at the school. She had a bank account. She had curvature of the spine. Buni and Ms. Tyson used to tell her to walk up straight. She used to walk bent over. That's the only way she could go fast. She could even run. She got tired of people telling her to walk up straight. She didn't like to do exercise. She did them with me but I could see she didn't really like to do them. She died at twenty-seven. That was a sad day when she died.

The reason I moved to Cheshire was for my son Calvin to go to Cheshire Academy. Calvin was born in 1951. I told my daughter Buni that the people in Cheshire wasn't going to like her. She said she would be fine. The first year we moved here was time for her to go to college. She went to Virginia for a couple of years and finished up at Quinnipiac College. When we first moved here people on the street put their house up for sale. But then we had one good neighbor, Mrs. McClain. The first day we moved here she came up and welcomed us, a wonderful lady. Every morning for forty years we would hear her car, she was going to church. We would be laying in the bed. We said that's Mrs. McClain. Well anyway, Calvin graduated from Cheshire Academy.

He said he wanted to be a preacher and so the summer before he went to college, he did a lot of work at Standard Beef. I knew the owner Hank. I had given him a lot of business when I worked for Reilly's, sometimes a hundred dollars a day. When I went into business for myself, Hank set me up. Calvin never went out with a black girl. He always went out with white girls. He was a happy man going to college. He had worked hard in the summer and bought all new clothes, suits and everything. He was a good kid. He used to come to Reilly's and I taught him how to cook. He used to help train the people.

My son went to college in Minnesota. When he got to college they put him in the room with a black guy from New York. Now this guy was out there to play basketball. He didn't like white people. My kid was there to go to college. One day my son was walking on campus with a white girl. That's all he knew was hanging with white people. When we went to Germany, that's what he did.

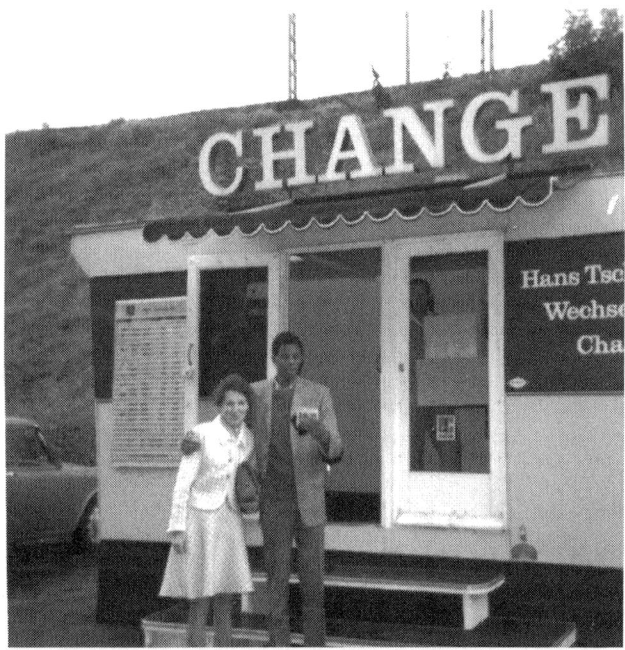

He never mingled with black people. He never went to New Haven because when he did, the black people didn't like him. I guess because he talked like white people. Anyway, he was walking on the campus with this white girl and they chastised him. The people at the school said you're not supposed to do that here. That same year he did not come home for Christmas. He stayed there. He came home in May. I met him at the airport In Hartford. He was standing right next to me at the airport and I didn't even recognize him. He had on a long overcoat from 1918. He didn't have a suitcase or nothing. By the time he came back from college he had been using drugs. He said he wasn't going back. He told the black guy what they had done to him and he said, I told you, I don't like white people. I really don't know what happened. He met a girl out there. They came here to our house. My wife didn't like her. She told Calvin he shouldn't be bothered with her. I guess the girl loved him. She lived in Boston. She called here and she came down. He used to meet her somewhere on the street because like I said my wife didn't like her. He decided to go to Boston to see her. He had a lot of money on him. He had been working. The captain from the police department called me from Boston and said he wanted to help my son. When he came back from Boston it looked like someone had beat him up. My son said the police had beat him up and taken his money. At that time black people didn't go into South Boston. When he came back he didn't seem right in his mind. He had met these guys. I guess they were selling drugs. I guess someone thought I was selling drugs. A plane used to come over my house. I guess they thought I had marijuana. One night someone called me on the phone and said Mr. Evans, I am over here on 84. I got a bag of cocaine. I didn't know anything about cocaine. I just listened to him. I said what they trying to do, set me up or something. I could stand in my backyard and see the people standing on the hill. He used to go with a girl back there. She was the daughter of the vice president at Yale. The same year he got back, he got a scholarship and went to Quinnipiac for a half year. Then he went to church and said he got the Holy Ghost. Then he decided to go back to school in Minnesota. I gave him a Volkswagen and he drove that Volkswagen all the way out there. He ended up in San Francisco and then in Los Angeles with my brother. My brother said something was sort of wrong with him. So I sent money out there and told my brother to send him home. He came home. I don't remember what happened to the car. Anyway, he came back and he and his mother were going to church. He also decided to go to broadcasting school in Hartford. I guess he wanted to be a DJ on the radio. He graduated from there In 1979.

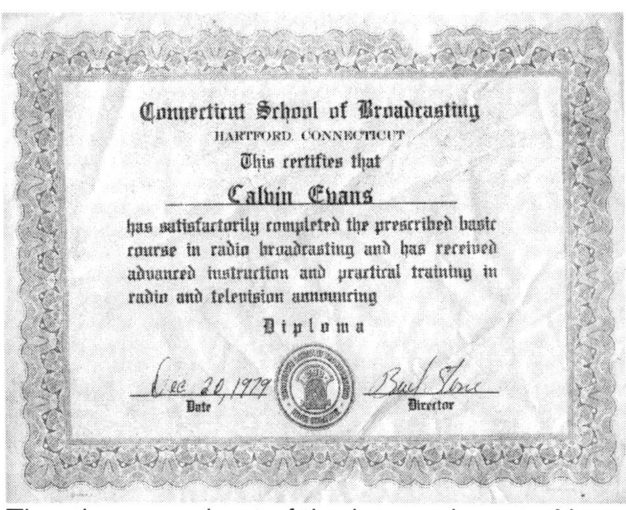
Connecticut School of Broadcasting
HARTFORD, CONNECTICUT
This certifies that
Calvin Evans
has satisfactorily completed the prescribed basic course in radio broadcasting and has received advanced instruction and practical training in radio and television announcing
Diploma
Dec 20, 1979
Date
Director

Then he moved out of the house down to New Haven on Grand Ave. My wife gave him a credit card, a visa credit card. He met these guys in New Haven who I guess scammed him out of his money. They put things on his visa card. My wife ended up paying for it. I remember the time when he died. Well, he came back home and he started going to church. I was happy for him. That night, it was on a Wednesday and I came home. He wanted some Maalox for an upset stomach. I took him to the drugstore right here in Cheshire and brought him back home. That Wednesday night, me and my wife were going to church. He was eating pork chops. We came back about 10:30 to 11:00. I was in my room and I heard a noise in his room. I said I would like to talk to Calvin. We met a nice member at the church and he was going to come out to see me and live with me for a couple of days. My wife said, don't bother him. He's sleeping or watching television. And so I didn't go in there, although I had heard something fall in there. The next morning I got up. Now he's generally up. He's usually cooking his own food. He supposed to be up. I said he's probably outside. Well, I got something to eat. Then when I went outside. I didn't see him out there. I forgot all about him. I came in went to the bathroom, washed up and got dressed. Now it's about 10:30,11:00. We were getting ready to go to church. We just fixing to walk out the door and my wife said, "Gee, we didn't even say goodbye to Calvin." I said do you think he is still sleeping? I was standing at the bathroom and she opened the door and she said, "Hey Calvin, we just wanted to see whether you were dead or alive. We getting ready to go to church." She looked in there and flipped the light on. He was laying up there, butt naked, all that stuff running out his nose. I looked at him. I didn't know what that stuff coming out his nose was. I said well he's alright, I guess. She said, "Calvin is dead, he's dead. I said, yeah, dead? I looked and I left. I called the cops. He had been to the doctor. He had some pills. He had enough pills to go 30 days. I guess he had been taking them for 15 days and had enough for another 15 days. They were pills to help keep him off cocaine. He had taken most of those pills at one time. They came and questioned me and took the rest of those pills. I wanted them to have an autopsy. He had so much of those pills in his system and that's what killed him. He was 220 lbs. and in top shape but that's what killed him. Well, I took a walk around the block and all around but that's what happened. Anyway, we buried him and that was it.

My oldest daughter is named Bunardy. We call her Buni. She was born in 1946. I remember when Reilly's restaurant burned down. The kids, Buni, Calvin and Dale wanted to give me the money back I had gave them for Christmas. They said you don't have a job now. I told them to keep their money. Buni went to Hillhouse High School in New Haven.

She was a majorette when she was there.

She was a beautiful girl growing up, but she was a bully. She didn't have many friends. She only had one friend in Brookside, a girl living across the street from us. Her name was Joan. Joan was a beautiful girl, but she died as a very young lady. Buni met Brack in high school. He used to play football in West Haven. He got hurt while he was playing. I thought Buni was going to have to take care of him for the rest of his life, but at that time they wasn't married.

He used to ask me when they got married was he doing the right thing. Was he taking care of my daughter good enough? Now some of the girls at school, they had a job. They were making money. Buni wanted to get a job, making money too. She didn't want to go to college. I told her you got to go to school. You got to learn something. So she signed up to go to school in Hampton, Virginia. After two years going to school in Virginia, she came home. She didn't want to go back. When she came from Virginia, she signed up to go to Quinnipiac college. I didn't know if she was going to go to college. Well, I wanted her to go to school. I didn't want her just to stick around here doing nothing. So I paid for her to go to computer school. So she ended up going to computer school and Quinnipiac college. She finished them both, did a great job. After that, she got a job with Blue Cross. Then she got a job with the Hartford insurance company. I couldn't understand it. She was always quitting a job. She said she had a job with Blue Cross with ten people working under her. She wanted to work with Brack. She was lazy. After all these years I begin to think about it. She was lazy. She didn't want to work in the yard. She wouldn't help me clean the yard. She didn't like bugs. She used to run in the house. She would always fight with Dale and Calvin. She fought with them all the time. My wife would tell me Buni and Calvin are always fighting. I would come home from work after 12 to 15 hours and she would tell me that. When Buni was a little girl, her mother used to fuss at them all the time. They didn't keep the room clean. She dominated her mother all the time. She wanted to do what she wanted to do.

When my wife was dying, Buni hardly visited her. She acted like she hated her mother, I don't know. It seemed like she tried to turn her mother against me. My wife told me, she said, "please don't give Buni nothing. Don't give Buni any of my money." Buni wanted her money. She came to the church and asked for the little bit of money she had.

We had a recession in the 1970's. I bought this house on Dixwell Avenue. Dr. Smith built this huge apartment building on Dixwell Avenue. With the recession, everything went down. Everything became cheap. You could buy a four family home for only thousands of dollars. Everything was so cheap. My son-in-law came to me and said we can buy this building on Dixwell Avenue for $60,000. We bought that apartment house in 1976 or 1977, just him and I. The building was huge. It had over 20 apartments in it. At this time I'm doing ok, doing pretty well. I'm working in New York and then I got a job in Rhode Island. He was taking care of everything. We made an agreement that we would make Cheshire our headquarters. But then because I was working so hard, I forgot all about that building. You know what, he sold that building. I had let them borrow money from me. He gave me a promissory note. I lent him $30,000. One time he paid me back with a bum check. I was going through some papers here in 2016. I was cleaning out my desk and I found this paper on my desk. I saw these papers where I had lent money to them like $10,000. One time I lent them $20,000 and they went on vacation. I remember when I was working at Reilly's, I would ride my bike to work and save my money. My wife told me that she was not going to pay any bills. She said that the man was supposed to pay the bills. So that's what I did. I told her to do what she wanted with her money. Well anyway, so I found this letter that was written by the lawyer of my daughter. Not too long ago this same lawyer came out here with my daughter. He was supposed to be coming out here to have me sign papers to sue a lady named Priscilla who owed me $5,000. I will tell you more about that later. My daughter had found the promissory note from Pricilla. It was laying on the table. My daughter saw it. She said, “I know this lady, a lawyer, Carolyn. This lady was trying to get some work from us. We were going to give her some business.” Buni went over to the hospital and told the people I was giving my money away. She told them I’m not capable of taking care of my money. So she bought the lawyer out here. I thought she was bringing the lawyer out here to sue Priscilla. I had told Buni if she got the money she could have it herself, the $5000. The lawyer starts reading off the stuff, telling me what he was going to do. He said you have to take this stuff to Cheshire and give it to the judge. When they ask you questions just say yes, yes, yes. I said why do I have to take it to Cheshire. I’ll take it to New Haven. He said you live in Cheshire. You have to take it to Cheshire. I said I’m not going to do it. I guess Buni got mad. This whole deal with the lawyer cost her $1500. What they were trying to do was get the power of attorney from me. If I signed what that man wanted me to sign, she would take every penny that I have. I ain’t going for that. Now this is the same lawyer who signed the paper when they sold the building on Dixwell Ave. I was shocked. I thought they were just coming out here to sue this lady. No, they wanted the power of attorney. They thought they was going to come out here and trick me and have the authority to take my house and take my money. They was going to tell the judge I'm giving my money away and turn everything over to her. That way they would have my houses, my money, everything. She was trying to become the power of attorney for me. She was trying to get the little bit of money that I had. I had already done everything for them. I helped put my grandchildren into school. Her daughter Jeanere, I gave her $10,000 to start Syracuse. I helped my grandson Brandon and I helped my grandson Brackston. I helped all of her children.

All three kids used to ask me to get on my bankbook. Anyway, by me going through all of my papers, I discovered a paper that said they had sold the building for $330,000.

DE BARBIERI & RUBIN
A PROFESSIONAL CORPORATION
ATTORNEYS AT LAW

KENNETH B. RUBIN
ROY L. DE BARBIERI

SARAH D. ELDRICH

MYRA DELAPP MOFFETT
OF COUNSEL

CAROL BESSA DENUZZO
OFFICE MANAGER
MARILYN R. GOLDBERG
PARALEGAL

458 SAW MILL ROAD
WEST HAVEN, CONNECTICUT 06516
(203) 934-3445

BRANCH
[illegible] YALE AVENUE
NEW HAVEN, CONNECTICUT [illegible]

REPLY TO WEST HAVEN

SELLER: BRACK G. POITIER AND JEFFREY EVANS

PROPERTY: 187 DIXWELL AVENUE, NEW HAVEN, CONNECTICUT

BUYER: 187 DIXWELL PLAZA, INC.

Purchase Price	$330,000.00
Less New Haven Savings Bank	47,000.00
	$283,000.00
Less Six Carpenters, Inc.	198,000.00
	$ 85,000.00
Less Commissioner of Revenue Services	1,800.00
	$ 83,200.00
Less Conveyance Tax	396.00
	$ 82,804.00
Less Recording Fees	15.00
	$ 82,789.00
Less Attorney's Fees	500.00
	$ 82,289.00
Less Jeffrey Evans	60,000.00 *
	$ 22,289.00

When we bought the building I put up $15,000. My son-in-law didn't have any money. Brack didn't have a penny. On this paper, it said they paid off the New Haven Savings Bank $47,000 and Six Carpenters got paid $198,000. Now Six Carpenters didn't have anything to do with the building. The paper said it paid off these different people you know like the clerks and things like that. The paper said they paid me $60,000. On the paper, it had my name wrong.

It said, Jeffrey Evans. They had sent me this letter. I never saw it before. I don't know how they slipped it into my business. Maybe I wasn't here and my wife put it in there, I don't know. I asked my daughter about it. I showed her the letter. Then I called Brack up and I said you owe me $60,000. Man he got mad, cussed me out and everything. He said man everybody wants to accuse me, saying I'm doing this and that. Man, I'm tired. Then he hung the phone up on me. My daughter said the letter was a phony. Buni said, well why are you talking about it now. I said well this letter is saying they gave me $60,000. I want to know what happened the money. Why did Six Carpenters get $198,000? It says the building got sold for $330,000. What happened to the money? She said, "well you got your $15,000 back didn't you?" I want to know what happened to the money. She said, well that's a phony. She said that's not real ,maybe they're just talking. They're just making up something. Well, I showed it to Dwane and he said he remembered that they sold the building to Harp. Dwane said I could go downtown, get the records and find out who sold the building and who signed the papers. Well, I went downtown and I found the papers.

To all People to Whom these Presents shall Come, Greeting:

Know Ye, That WE, BRACK G. POITIER, of Hamden, Connecticut, and JEFFERSON EVANS, of Cheshire, Connecticut,

for the consideration of THREE HUNDRED THIRTY THOUSAND DOLLARS ($330,000.00) *received to* our *full satisfaction of* ONE EIGHTY SEVEN DIXWELL PLAZA, INC., a Connecticut corporation doing business in New Haven, Connecticut

do give, grant, bargain, sell and confirm unto the said ONE EIGHTY SEVEN DIXWELL PLAZA, INC.

ALL THAT CERTAIN place or parcel of land situated in the Town and County of New Haven and State of Connecticut and known as Reuse Parcel 2A of the Dixwell Redevelopment and Renewal Area. Containing 47,159 square feet, more or less, and bounded and described as follows:

Beginning at the Northeasterly corner of Dixwell Avenue and Foote Street, said point being North 176,593.46 feet and East 549,469.05 on the Connecticut Geodetic Grid System;

Thence proceeding North 78 degrees, 42 minutes, 03 seconds East 313.13 feet along the Northerly line of Foote Street;

Thence proceeding North 11 degrees, 35 minutes, 09 seconds West 150.81 feet along land belonging now or formerly to New Haven Housing Authority;

Thence proceeding South 78 degrees, 42 minutes, 07 seconds West 312.27 feet along land belonging now or formerly to the City of New Haven;

Thence proceeding South 11 degrees, 15 minutes, 46 seconds East 150.81 feet along the Easterly line of Dixwell Avenue to point and place of beginning.

Said premises are subject to building lines, if established, all laws, ordinances or governmental regulations, including all building and zoning ordinances affecting said premises; and taxes to the Town of New Haven on the List of October 1, 1985, not yet due and payable, which the grantee herein assumes and agrees to pay as part of the consideration for this deed.

Said premises are also subject to utility easements, restrictions, and agreements appearing of record.

1650.00 CONVEYANCE TAX RECEIVED

$ 363.00 CONVEYANCE TAX RECEIVED

To Have and to Hold *the above granted and bargained premises, with the appurtenances thereof, unto* it *the said grantee* its successors ~~heirs~~ *and assigns forever, to and their own proper use and behoof. And also,* we *the said grantors do for* our selves our *heirs, executors, and administrators, covenant with the said grantee* its successors ~~heirs~~ *and assigns, that at and until the ensealing of these presents,* we are *well seized of the premises, as a good indefeasible estate in FEE SIMPLE; and have good right to bargain and sell the same in manner and form as is above written; and that the same is free from all incumbrances whatsoever, except as above stated.*

I Got The Proof.

Grid System;

Thence proceeding North 78 degrees, 42 minutes, 03 seconds East 313.13 feet along the Northerly line of Foote Street;

Thence proceeding North 11 degrees, 35 minutes, 09 seconds West 150.81 feet along land belonging now or formerly to New Haven Housing Authority;

Thence proceeding South 78 degrees, 42 minutes, 07 seconds West 312.27 feet along land belonging now or formerly to the City of New Haven;

Thence proceeding South 11 degrees, 15 minutes, 46 seconds East 150.81 feet along the Easterly line of Dixwell Avenue to point and place of beginning.

Said premises are subject to building lines, if established, all laws, ordinances or governmental regulations, including all building and zoning ordinances affecting said premises; and taxes to the Town of New Haven on the List of October 1, 1985, not yet due and payable, which the grantee herein assumes and agrees to pay as part of the consideration for this deed.

Said premises are also subject to utility easements, restrictions, and agreements appearing of record.

1650.00 CONVEYANCE TAX RECEIVED

$ 363.00 CONVEYANCE TAX RECEIVED

To Have and to Hold *the above granted and bargained premises, with the appurtenances thereof, unto* it *the said grantee* its successors ~~heirs~~ *and assigns forever, to and their own proper use and behoof. And also,* we *the said grantors do for* ourselves our *heirs, executors, and administrators, covenant with the said grantee* its successors ~~heirs~~ *and assigns, that at and until the ensealing of these presents,* we are *well seized of the premises, as a good indefeasible estate in FEE SIMPLE; and have good right to bargain and sell the same in manner and form as is above written; and that the same is free from all incumbrances whatsoever, except as above stated.*

And Furthermore, we *the said grantors do by these presents bind* ourselves *and* our *heirs forever to WARRANT AND DEFEND the above granted and bargained premises to* it *the said grantee* its successors ~~heirs~~ *and assigns, against all claims and demands whatsoever, except as above stated.*

In Witness Whereof, we *have hereunto set* our *hand s and seal s* ~~[struck-out text]~~ *this* 20th *day of* May *1976.*

Signed, Sealed and Delivered in the presence of

Roy L. DeBarbieri — Brack G. Poitier *(L.S.)*

Sarah J. Eldrich — Jefferson Evans *(L.S.)*

(L.S.)

(L.S.)

Four people signed the papers. Someone signed my name. He got $330,000 for that building. And I didn't get nothing for that building except my $15,000 back. Now I always thought that the white people out here hated my guts. They treated me bad. The reason I said that is because when I got here everybody on the street put their house up for sale. They didn't want me out here. They burnt a cross on my lawn. They used to put garbage on my lawn. They did all kinds of things. I bought a new snow blower and I shoveled the snow for a lady one day and she came out cussing me out. They did everything. I couldn't understand why they were like this. Then I thought about my family. My family, Brack and my daughter treated me worse than the white people ever treated me. I called my daughter up and said I got the proof. She started yelling and saying how I was treating her bad. I said I got the proof. Come on out here and look at this. This paper shows that Brack sold the building for $330,000 and somebody signed my name. I got the proof. She hung up and that was about a week ago. She has not called me back in about a week. About a week before that, I gave her $5000. She went down to the bank and cashed the check. Then she had the bank people to put her name on the bank book. I told her when she asked me, I said I don't want your name on that bank book. She went down there and did it anyway. She knew this lady who went to the church that worked at the bank. She told her what to do. But when they sent me those checks with Buni's name on it. I got mad. I told her I said I told you not to put your name on the bank book. I went down there the next day and I took it off. Anyway, I want to see what Brack is going to say after he gets the proof. I want him to tell me what he did with the money. They know I got the proof. That's why they wouldn't even pick up the phone. I want him to tell me who signed all those names on it. I need that money. He treated me like a jackass. I figured he was my son-in-law. He talking about he's going to have nothing to do with this. I'm going to talk to the lawyer. Whatever the Lord tells me, that's what's going to happen. It is going to be all over. If my lawyer tells me he can't do anything, it's going to be all over. But I still want to know. The lawyer is going to send him letters. He's going to ask him what happened to the money. I want to know. Let Brack tell the story. Why he did that. What he did with the money. Why did he do it? I did everything for them. I called Brack and he never answered the phone. I ask the question again. **Why do people treat me the way they do?** Well, I have to get more copies. I want to show it to the bishop. They hang around the bishop now. I'm going to say you have con artists hanging around you.

Earlier this year, Brack asked me for 230,000. He said he needed it and he was going to make me a millionaire. He said he wanted to use the money to pay the IRS and some other things. He showed me some properties. One of the houses was in Hamden up on some rocks. When we came back to the house he said in a rough voice, "ARE YOU GOING TO GIVE ME THE MONEY?" I told him I wanted to meet with him and Buni. When they came to the house, I talked about a lot of things. I got a lot of stuff off my chest. I asked

Buni about the time her son came over yelling at me. My grandson Brackston came out here cussing me out. He said his mother said that I called his grandmother a whore. That's the worst thing anybody could say to someone. He called me every name in the book. I was scared. Again I ask, **why do people treat me the way they do?** They said it didn't happen. I had a chance to tell Buni and Brack about other things on my mind. I didn't give them nothing. This is 2016 and I talked to my lawyer. He said he can't do anything because he has represented Brack and Buni before. It would be a conflict of interest. He said he could lose his license. The lawyer said he talked with Buni. He said she told him the reason they did it was because at that time they didn't have any work. They needed money so they sold the building. He said I could probably get another lawyer. He asked me did I sign the deed for the sale. I said no. He said something about fraud. I still haven't talked to Buni since I told her that I got the proof. That was almost two weeks ago. I found out that the people who bought the building from Brack sold it about two years later for $840,000.

THIS AGREEMENT made between 187 DIXWELL PLAZA, INC., a Connecticut corporation, with its office and principal place of business in the Town and County of New Haven and State of Connecticut, hereinafter called the SELLER; and JONATHAN A. BANQUER, of the Town of Branford, County of New Haven and State of Connecticut, hereinafter called the BUYER; as follows:

1. SELLER agrees to sell and BUYER agrees to buy for the sum of EIGHT HUNDRED FORTY THOUSAND and no/100 DOLLARS ($840,000.00) certain property in New Haven, Connecticut, known as 187 Dixwell Avenue, all as more specifically described in Schedule A appended hereto, with all the buildings and other improvements and all appurtenances thereto, including all leases and personal property and fixtures therein, in their present condition.

2. The purchase price is payable as follows:

(a) By deposit on Seller's acceptance, to be held in escrow by SELLER'S attorney until closing : $10,000.00

(b) By cash or certified check at closing, subject to the expenses and adjustments herein: $830,000.00

TOTAL.. $840,000.00

3. The BUYER has examined said property and is satisfied with the physical condition thereof, and neither SELLER nor any agent of SELLER has made any representation or promise other than those expressly stated herein upon which the BUYER has relied in making this agreement.

4. SELLER warrants and represents that the subject premises consist of a legally zoned, twenty-four (24) unit residential apartment building; that he has no knowledge of any impending mechanic's liens or other threatened litigation concerning the premises; that no tenant, lessee or occupant has prepaid rent for a period in excess of thirty (30) days; that no tenant, lessee or occupant has any known defense, set-off or counterclaim to any lease or other obligation; that the Seller has not been cited for any uncorrected building, fire, handicapped and/or other codes known to the Seller; and, that there are no outstanding options to purchase and/or options affecting said premises.

5. All risk of loss or damage to said property by fire, theft or other casualty until delivery of the deed shall be on the SELLER and SELLER shall insure said property in appropriate amounts. In the event of substantial damage to the property, BUYER shall, within 30 days of notice to him of such damage, elect either to receive any insurance payable on account of such damage and proceed to take title; or, rescind this agreement and receive back all amounts theretofore paid on account of the purchase price in which event all rights under this agreement shall terminate.

6. Taxes, fuel oil, utilities, rent, sewer use payments and like matters shall be adjusted pro rata, and rent security deposits and interest thereon, shall be credited to the BUYER as of the date the deed is delivered; further, similar adjustment shall be made with regard to any insurance policies and service contracts which BUYER may agree to assume. The tax adjustment shall be made in accordance with the customary New Haven method, as opposed to a "uniform fiscal year" method.

7. The premises to be conveyed shall include all fixtures presently on the premises, plumbing, heating and lighting fixtures, and the like; all kitchen appliances owned by the Seller and other items of personal property in, on and about the premises which is appurtenant to the premises or used in the operation of the premises, which personal property shall be free and clear of any security interests or other encumbrances. SELLER shall provide BUYER with a bill of sale with usual covenants and warranties at closing. A list of the personal propety shall be provided to the BUYER by SELLER within ten (10) days after the receipt by Seller of notice of a firm bank commitment to the Buyer.

8. The SELLER represents and warrants that attached hereto as **Schedule B** is an accurate schedule of all leases and tenancies affecting said premises and an accurate schedule of cash flow provided by the premises; also, an accurate statement of operating expenses during the past one (1) year, except for maintenance costs. SELLER represents that all of the leases are in full force and effect and that all tenants are in possession unless otherwise noted therein.

9. BUYER'S obligations hereunder are contingent on BUYER'S obtaining mortgage financing in an amount of not less than Eight Hundred Ten Thousand and no/100 Dollars ($810,000.00), at current interest rates for commercial transactions similar to this,

I love my daughter, but I'm still mad. I can't believe how they treated me. **Why do people treat me the way they do?** By the way, My grandchildren are doing good. Baron is a preacher. Jeanere is a nurse and Brackston is building houses. Jeanere has two children and Baron has three children.

Chapter 10
Telling The Truth Is Hard

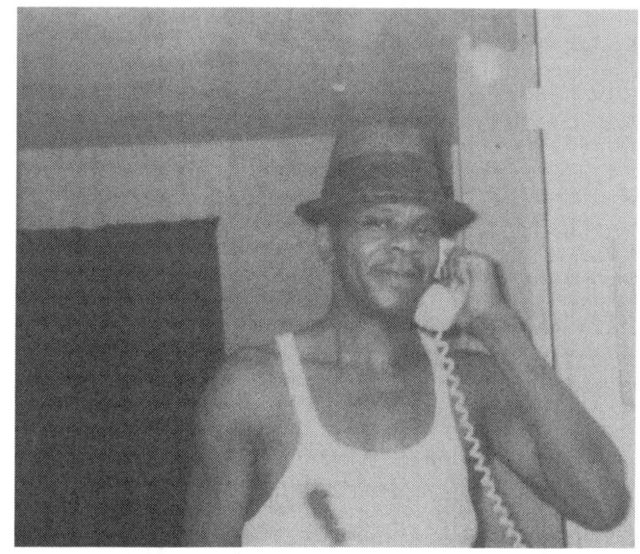

When I started to write this book, some things that I did, I know wasn't right. I didn't want to do it. But if you going to write a book about your life. You should tell the truth, nothing but the truth. I thought about that. Well, this is the hardest part for me to say. We all did bad things during our lifetime. Well if you want to call this bad. When you are a kid, twelve, thirteen years old. You get up in the morning and by the time you go to bed you have a hard on all night. You don't care what you do. You might grab your sister and try. But if they're mean, you don't try anymore. You might try the chicken if you can get it in there. You might try a dog. Well the cow, they won't stand still long enough. Everybody does something bad during their lifetime. Well, I used to plow this mule. She can't have kids, she can't have mules. Anyway, I had a mule. This mule got to know me. My brother showed me things about my body. This is hard. I didn't know there was no Santa Claus. He told me there was no Santa Claus. I got mad. I went and told my mother. He said look what's coming out of me, white stuff. He felt good after it came out. Well, I don't know how I tried to do it with this mule. We had five horses. Each one had a stall. They were smart. They knew which stall to go in. When you step over the door you go down a little bit. When you get ready to feed your mule she walks down. I'm not sure how it happened, but every time I would go in the mule would be facing me, then she would turn around and get right to the door. Then I step to the door and stick it right into her. She got one just like a woman. I used to do that all the time. Stick it in there and go up and down. My brother, well I don't know if my brother used to do it. I don't know if my father knew I used to do it. My father, he did bad things too. Everybody did bad things. My father, he was a good man. He was honest but he went into a store one day and grabbed a hat when the man wasn't looking and put it in his bosom. Well, this mule, when I went in, used to turn around and come right to the door. She used to put her butt right up to the door. She knew what she wanted and she was happy. I shouldn't say this but I did it. When you're a boy you do a lot of things. Well, I'm saying this because if you are going to write a book of your life you have to tell it all. It wouldn't be right not to tell this. That's the worst thing that I ever did. Before I got married, I used to do women every night. I had a woman one time, that's all she wanted to do all night long. When you are young, you never get soft and that's what she wanted. She wanted to go all night. I did a lot of bad things, but if you are going to write a book, you tell it. There was an old lady who said to me, you should go with my daughter and she was holy. She was sanctified, a preacher's wife. The bishop, when I was going to church, he used to talk about things like that. He said I wouldn't trust another man with my wife, women they do anything.

That's life. But since I been married, I never went to another woman. I been married all these years. I believed that God would have done something to me. I was true to my wife. But my wife, I know she went to different people. I know one time she laid up in the bed with this man, my brother. I know that. I was downstairs. Then she came running downstairs to me with this little short dress on saying that she's sorry. I didn't say anything. I could have left her, but why should I break up my marriage, break up my life. I told my wife if you want to do it, go head. I told guys if you tell my wife she looks good, she will probably go to bed with you. A lot of people get mad, kill people about a woman. I said to myself, why should I go to court, fight, lose my home and lose everything. I knew she laid up in the bed. I didn't care. It's still there. If she gave me a disease or something, I might kill her. But it's still there and I knew she still loved me. You love people, but you see something you like and you get it. If it costs you money you get it, but I never went to another woman while I was with my wife. I knew it was wrong. The bible said it was wrong and I never did it. I think that's one of the reasons why God shows me so much now. Everybody tells me I'm different and yeah I am different. I see things different. One day I am going to overcome my knees. I think that God is one day going to strengthen my knees. I can do things right now. Anyway, I wanted to say that. It was hard for me to say what I just said, but if you are going to do something, tell the truth. Don't be a liar. Don't mix up things. Tell the truth. Everything I'm saying about my life is true. I'm happy for that. If you tell the truth, you'll be blessed. I don't care what you do and that's me. God Bless you.

Chapter 11

Is It Just A Scam?

My wife had died in December 2013. At this time in my life, I was very confused. I started to drinking cold water and carrot juice. I must of drank at least a gallon a day between the two. The carrot juice had made my wife feel good, so I would feel good too. Then my leg used to get water blisters. It had nowhere to go. Now this guy had started to come over. I knew him over the years. He had a couple of daughters. His name was Moses. He came from New Haven. He showed a lot of interest in my wife when she was sick. I used to treat him nice, give him money and dinners. I did it from my heart. I said here's a man that likes me that well,the to come out to shovel my snow. I would give him fifty, a hundred dollars to shovel and he claimed he liked me. Well, one day my daughter had come by and saw the blisters on my leg. She didn't know what to do so she said we will put a bandage on it. Moses happened to come by and he said, man, you got to go the hospital. He said, "I'll take you." That's when I started going to the VA Hospital. They looked at it and they wrapped it up. After they wrapped it up I went home. They sent a nurse in two days to my house to change the bandage on it. She wouldn't change the bandage on it. She said that you should go back there and let them do it. She didn't think something was right. I went back to the VA and they kept me there for three days. Moses was there. He had been coming to the house and visiting my wife. He said man, "You was going to die. Your leg was going to get bad," and all that. Like I said I had been paying him to shovel the snow and stuff like that. One time we was out shoveling snow. He was helping me and I fell down in the snow. He helped me get up. He would always remind me and say if he didn't help me I would have died. Anyway all of a sudden in March, he comes up to me and he wants to borrow five thousand dollars. I was skeptical and I asked him was it a scam. "Why have you been so nice to me? That's what you wanted, to get my money?" He answered in a nice voice. He said "well if you can do it, I want to get into this type of business. If you can do it, it would be nice, if you can't you just can't," all in a nice voice. I said gee, this guy been with me all these years and he's nice and he never asked me for nothing. I said what the hell is five thousand dollars. So I said, "You write up the slip and tell me when you're going to pay me back and I'll give it to you." The next day he came and we went to the bank and got the five thousand dollars. Around that time I had an invention that I had started and I asked him could he help me. I told him I would like him to go there and listen to this guy. I should have gotten this thing going at the beginning of the year, but here it is March and I haven't heard from this guy. I don't want you to say anything, just listen. The guy called me in March and hung up on me. He said I had lied and he told me I had not done the right thing. He said I kept changing my mind because I had two inventions. I was making carrot juice and I had an invention to help old people like me called Jeff's Reach Easy. I guess I told Moses I would make him partners. Moses said I'll go and he went with me. He told the guy, he said, maybe you and Jeff don't understand each other. I told the guy this is not my money I am giving you. I had given him about thirty thousand dollars. I told the guy this was the organization's money. Moses was supposed to be part of the organization. Moses was a smart guy. I liked him. He started writing letters to the district attorney, consumer groups. He just knew what to do. I wanted somebody to write a letter to the nursing home on Whitney Ave that they had killed my wife and he did that. He didn't do exactly what I told him to do but at the time whatever he did I thought he was a wonderful man. He kept taking me to the VA. Now I'm going to the VA for my knees. I wanted a second opinion about my knees. It took from March to July 24th to get an opinion. They checked my blood pressure. They checked my heart. They said something is wrong with my heart. They said I'm going to die. They did everything. Put all kinds of things on me. I was telling Moses what they said. He said, man, if it wasn't for me you would have died. He tried to turn me against my family. He said they wasn't helping you. I said to myself, I'm in a losing world, what can I do. He said they don't care about you. You should get rid of them. Then I put his name on my bank book. I told him if something happened to me now, they wouldn't give you a nickel. It was to give him understanding that what he was doing, I didn't want him to do it for nothing. We didn't want my daughter to know but she read it and she crossed the name off. Then I had something to get back at her. When my wife was in the hospital she used to pay this girl to come out there. I told her that you don't have to pay anybody to give my wife water. I asked how much do you pay this girl. The girl used to come from twelve to five. She said I give her ten dollars an hour. Now that was 50 dollars every day for forty-one days. I said you don't have to do that. She looked at me and said, "It's my money, I'll do what I want to do with it." I said ok, I didn't say nothing. So then when she crossed the name off the bank book, I asked her why did you cross that name off. She didn't say anything. I said I'll tell you like you told me, "This is my money and I'll do what I want with it." She had nothing to say. Well, everything was going good. I was sort of happy with the invention thing. Moses had written a lot of letters so this guy had gotten a little scared. He called me and said he wanted to give me my money back. I said I didn't want the money back and that he would have to talk to Moses. He sent me the check around the beginning of June. He kept my money all that time and didn't give me no interest. So I ask, **"Why do people treat me the way they do?"**

49 Green Hill Lane
Cheshire, CT 06410

June 16, 2014

Armando Ortiz
Regional Sales Director
InventHelp
57 Plains Road
Suite 1A
Milford, CT 06461

RE: File # CTO-636-601 U

Dear Mr. Ortiz:

I am in receipt of your money order # 14019768 for $27,000, which I imagine indicates that you have decided to discontinue our relationship.

Mr. Ortiz, I find this to be unacceptable for several reasons:

1. The $27,000 that you have refunded does not include all expenses paid as a result of the endeavor with InventHelp. There remain a $199 fee for Preliminary Patentability Search and Opinion, as well as a $945 fee for service(s) purchased BIP Search. Therefore the total outstanding balance owed by InventHelp is $1,144.00. See attached.

2. Our agreement for service was initiated on 10/29/2013 during which you outlined the turn of events that were to have taken place within the next 5 months. The 11/14/2013 letter from InventHelp clearly implied that progressive work had been done on my file, as evidence by the Basic Information Package (outlining production, marketing and promotional considerations). Once you received your referred Patent Attorney's Professional Opinion you were immediately going to submit an application to the U.S. patent Office.

   I considered this to have been fantastic news because patent approval would/should have expedited the production process. Unfortunately in our 3/6/2014 meeting with you, me and my partner Moses you presented a completely different agenda. Although I was visibly upset with what I considered to have been your blatant misrepresentation, Moses wanted to give you the benefit of the doubt and grant you the time requested. With such you specifically Assured us that you would receive a response from the patent office by 5/31/2014 and prepare a short-list of selected manufacturers.

   Moses clearly recognized the gap in communication and corresponded with you on several occasion (by mail, e-mail and phone) as of today you have yet to respond. Unfortunately your neglect merely foster my opinion of your unscrupulous behavior while professing to provide the services necessary to complete the production and marketing of my JEFF'S EASY REACH invention.

3. The Preliminary Patentability Search and Opinion displays several similar product with an approved patent. Your referred patent attorney's professional opinion outlined in his 12/3/2013 letter that patent protection of JEFF"S EASY REACH should be available. Measured against similar marketable products, I can only imagine what would be the projected sales of JEFF"S EASY REACH, which now amounts to a significant profit loss.

   Mr. Moses's 4/16/2014 e-mail to you specifically requested an explanation for your abrupt decision. In the middle of this turmoil I expect InventHelp to honor any/all privacy agreement as well as protecting my proprietary rights. In an attempt to avoid a litigated acceleration of this matter I expect to receive a response (by 6/23/2014) to all request made to you in Mr. Moses correspondence, particularly your reasoning for severing our relationship.

Your cooperative assistance on this matter is appreciated.

Sincerely

Jefferson Evans

CC: Connecticut Department of Consumer Protection
Connecticut Department of Banking
Federal Trade Commission

Before that time, somewhere in May, Moses had asked me for another 500 dollars which I gave him. Now it was near the first of July and he asked me for another 500 dollars. He was supposed to be paying the five thousand back at the beginning of August. I knew to myself if I continue to give him money, he's going to keep asking. I put gas in his car. When I go in a store and I buy something and I say put in on my bill. I said well we got the money back from the invention, but we can sue him because he held my money for eight months without giving me anything. Moses mentioned if it had been a lawyer, the lawyer would have gotten a third. So I said what I am going to do is give you a third. He had been riding me around and they was going to cut my leg off. He had been brainwashing me and I had forgot I had told him I was going to make him a partner in the invention. I said well I'm going to give you another five thousand. I said I'm going to give you a third. I sat down at the table and wrote it out. I said the first five thousand, I'll cross it out. Now I'm going to give you another five thousand. That will be a third. I wrote the check. He said well it should be, he kinda mumbled. I said you seem not to be happy with what I'm doing. So altogether I had given him ten thousand five hundred dollars. He didn't really seem happy. I had told him at the beginning it was a scam. I had given the first five thousand for taking me around. I had given it to him so he can have some cash money in and the last five thousand for the invention. Now the next day we had to go the doctor. He came here at nine o'clock. We went to BJ's , that's where we get the gas. He said I'm going to get five dollars worth of gas, that's all the money I got. Ok, we went to the doctor and we came back to BJ's. He said I'll take your credit card and I'll fill up the tank. Now I was skeptical because he had the five thousand in his hand. I didn't want to give it to him, but he said in that voice again, "if you don't want to give it to me, it's alright. It's alright." Then I gave him my discover card and he filled the tank up. The next day he came to my house at nine o'clock. I asked him did he have a BJ card. He said yeah, I got a card. I said "Get the hell out of my house. You are a scam. I said if you weren't a scam, why would you ask me to fill your tank up and you had five thousand dollars in your hand. You had the money, you could have paid for it. I said get the hell out of my house, you're nothing but a scam. I told you that at the beginning." He said, "do you want me to take you to the doctor today?" I said, "if you tell me why you did that, if it's not a scam, I'll tell you if I want you to take me to the doctor." He talked and complained and he talked. Then he said to me, "huh, you old man talking to me like this." And that's what hit me hard. I said now if he had said to me like he did before in that voice, I'm sorry, I forgot, I wasn't thinking and I'm having a lot of problems. If he had said something like that, I would have known, he could have gotten everything I had, my house and everything. I just told him to get the hell out of my house. I don't want you to do anything for me. You did everything wrong. You are a scam artist. The doctor at the office asked me when I went there in July, he said where's your buddy. I told him I got rid of him. I ended up telling the doctor what happened. He said, see, I knew that. He said I was skeptical of him. They get these old people and they try to get what they got. Well, I did it in an honest way. I was happy. He did a good job. He claimed he saved my life but I know that wasn't true. If somebody does something for me, I want to pay them. But I had told him, he didn't have to do all those things. I told him the people at the VA would do those things themselves. I told him at the beginning. Moses called me and I told him I had been over there a couple of days. I go through the valet thing. They take me out. I tell them I need a wheelchair, they get it and take me to the doctor. I said, I told you but you didn't listen. He keeps calling me. I see it on the caller id. I don't want no part of him. He's a crook. I told him he's a lousy crook. But what I did for him, I would do for anybody. I'm not sorry that I did it. I'm just sorry that he lied to me. That's the only thing that hurts me for a man to lie to me and tell me he's helping me and I'm through with him. I hope I never see him again I wouldn't give a darn. Here is my question. **Why do people treat me the way they do?**

You try to do your best. I've been living here for maybe 52, 53 years. This a story about a lady, her name is Priscilla. The first time she came she was asking for about seventy thousand dollars. She had about three or four houses she was about to lose that she couldn't pay for. Glenn was here listening trying to help explain things. I couldn't help her. I wanted to introduce her to my son-in-law. He said he couldn't help her. Five or six months later she came back. She bought this lawyer out here. Her name is Carolyn. I asked Glenn to come back out her to listen again. Glenn and the lawyer was the negotiators for her and she promised to do everything. She wanted five thousand dollars and she was supposed to come pick me up once a week or four times a month. The lawyer was supposed to fill out a paper with the deal. She was supposed to pay me my money back in a year. That was in July. We gave her three months before she was supposed to make the first payment. She was supposed to come get me the next week. I made dinner for them in a few days. Priscilla called me up in about two weeks. She said this is very serious. I got to talk to you right away. She didn't want anybody else to come this time. I called Glenn to come anyway. When she got here she said I need two thousand dollars, I need two thousand dollars. We asked her why did she need another two thousand dollars. She said she couldn't pay back the five thousand unless she got the two thousand. I was shocked that she wanted money that fast. I didn't give her anything. I didn't hear from her for two or three months. I called her and she called me back and she said she wanted to take me places. She said she had been sick in the hospital. I asked her why she hadn't called me in three months. She came and took me to the store. The next time she took me to get my flu shot at Walgreens. We sat there for an hour. She started turning the car around out of the driveway and she said I need gas money. I'm gonna run out before I get can get anyplace. I can't go all the way out there and come back. She said I need gas, do you have money to give me gas. I didn't say anything. I did say I have two dollars to give her. She said that's not enough money to get a gallon of gas. We drove down Whitney Ave. and she start talking. I didn't say any more about the gas. Well, she started to come over and take me places to the store, stuff like that. She still didn't pay me any money. She say we could go out for dinner and music and stuff like that. When she called me I told her I had a contract with her. We could not mix business with pleasure with the contract. We talked and I did like talking with her . We talked about things from the past, but I didn't walk to mix the business I had with her. Then she start talking about her condo in Branford. She said she was going to lose it if she didn't get ten thousand dollars. I didn't trust her and I told her that she never did what she was supposed to do. If she had did what she was supposed to do, she could have gotten anything. We probably could be buddies. She kept talking about losing the condo. She said someone wanted to buy it for 75 thousand dollars but she had to pay ten thousand dollars before she could sell it. She said he was trying to get more for it than that. She talked about this every time she came over. She got mad with me another time when she said she need gas money. I didn't give her anything. One day she gave me a check for 300 dollars and took me to the bank. I put the check into my account. that was the only money she gave me from what she owed me. That was in, I think February or March that she gave me that money. Anyway, she kept talking about the condo and I guess I felt sorry for her. She said when she sold it she would give me back my five thousand dollars she owed me if I would give her the ten thousand. She would give me all of it back plus interest, another two thousand dollars. I felt sorry for her so I told her I would help her. But then when the time came she lied. We told her she needed to show us the paperwork for the sale and who was giving me my money back. She had a lawyer who called me and he said he could not guarantee me my money and he wasn't sure about who was going to buy it. She just lied to me so I did not help her. I even told her I would buy the condo for 75 thousand just to get rid of her but she didn't want to sell it to me. So I didn't give her a dime and she still hasn't paid me. She ended up losing the condo. I am suing her for my five thousand dollars. Right now I have to go to court for this.

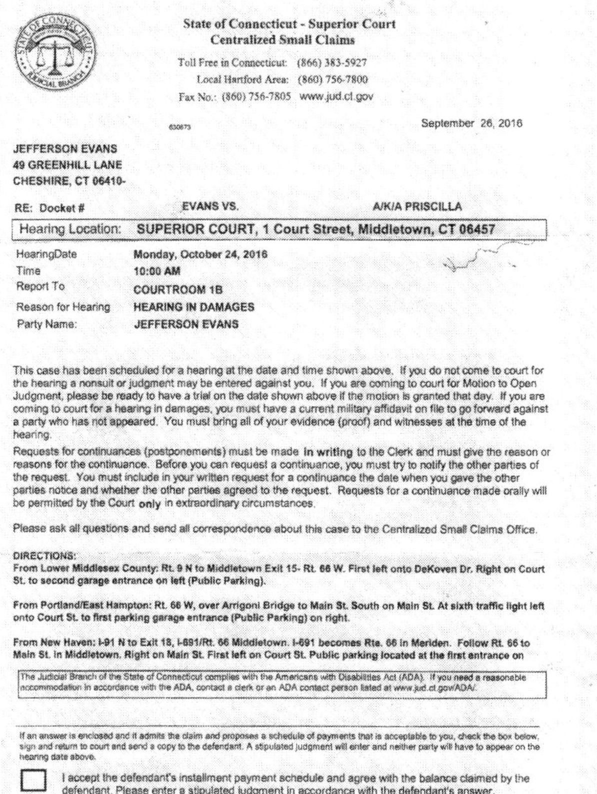

State of Connecticut - Superior Court
Centralized Small Claims

Toll Free in Connecticut: (866) 383-5927
Local Hartford Area: (860) 756-7800
Fax No.: (860) 756-7805 www.jud.ct.gov

630873

September 26, 2016

JEFFERSON EVANS
49 GREENHILL LANE
CHESHIRE, CT 06410-

RE: Docket # EVANS VS. A/K/A PRISCILLA

Hearing Location: **SUPERIOR COURT, 1 Court Street, Middletown, CT 06457**

HearingDate	**Monday, October 24, 2016**
Time	**10:00 AM**
Report To	**COURTROOM 1B**
Reason for Hearing	**HEARING IN DAMAGES**
Party Name:	**JEFFERSON EVANS**

This case has been scheduled for a hearing at the date and time shown above. If you do not come to court for the hearing a nonsuit or judgment may be entered against you. If you are coming to court for Motion to Open Judgment, please be ready to have a trial on the date shown above if the motion is granted that day. If you are coming to court for a hearing in damages, you must have a current military affidavit on file to go forward against a party who has not appeared. You must bring all of your evidence (proof) and witnesses at the time of the hearing.

Requests for continuances (postponements) must be made **in writing** to the Clerk and must give the reason or reasons for the continuance. Before you can request a continuance, you must try to notify the other parties of the request. You must include in your written request for a continuance the date when you gave the other parties notice and whether the other parties agreed to the request. Requests for a continuance made orally will be permitted by the Court **only** in extraordinary circumstances.

Please ask all questions and send all correspondence about this case to the Centralized Small Claims Office.

DIRECTIONS:
From Lower Middlesex County: Rt. 9 N to Middletown Exit 15- Rt. 66 W. First left onto DeKoven Dr. Right on Court St. to second garage entrance on left (Public Parking).

From Portland/East Hampton: Rt. 66 W, over Arrigoni Bridge to Main St. South on Main St. At sixth traffic light left onto Court St. to first parking garage entrance (Public Parking) on right.

From New Haven: I-91 N to Exit 18, I-691/Rt. 66 Middletown. I-691 becomes Rte. 66 in Meriden. Follow Rt. 66 to Main St. in Middletown. Right on Main St. First left on Court St. Public parking located at the first entrance on

The Judicial Branch of the State of Connecticut complies with the Americans with Disabilities Act (ADA). If you need a reasonable accommodation in accordance with the ADA, contact a clerk or an ADA contact person listed at www.jud.ct.gov/ADA/.

If an answer is enclosed and it admits the claim and proposes a schedule of payments that is acceptable to you, check the box below, sign and return to court and send a copy to the defendant. A stipulated judgment will enter and neither party will have to appear on the hearing date above.

☐ I accept the defendant's installment payment schedule and agree with the balance claimed by the defendant. Please enter a stipulated judgment in accordance with the defendant's answer.

Signed ....
Plaintiff/Plaintiff Attorney

Notice of Court Hearing
JD-CV-40 H1
Revised 9/2012

She sent me a paper from the court saying she will pay me back ten dollars a week. I have to ask the question. **Why do people treat me the way they do?** The court decided she would have to pay me thirty-five dollars a week starting in November 2016.

I thought that I had gotten rid of Dwane. I dealt with Dwane 20 years ago. I met Dwane through Brack and Six Carpenters. Six Carpenters did home improvement. Dwane used to work with them. That's how I met Dwane. He was a young fellow. Brack was maybe 10 or 15 years older than Dwane. They said he was lazy. He didn't want to work. Then I met him. I liked him. I treated him like he was my son. Dwane wanted to be like Brack, Bill and Lynch. Dwane, I thought he was pretty smart. I offered to give him my restaurant but he didn't want it. His wife did not show any interest in it. I must've met him when he was in his teens, maybe 20 something. I bought a house on Hurlburt Street. Dwane had lost the house. I didn't want it. I told him we could get it together. At first, my wife didn't want her name on the deed. Anyway when I was about to buy the house, Dwane went away for a couple weeks. When he came back he said did you buy the house. I said yeah. He said well we have to go and put my name on it. I went over to the lawyer's office and she said, you must be crazy. Then Dwane went out and told people that I stole the house, but I didn't buy it from him. He lost the house. I bought the house for $20,000. I still have the house today. This is where I ask the question. **Why do people treat me the way they do?** Well, I worked with him for about three or four years. After that I let him go. I told him I didn't want to be bothered with him. I told him he wasn't making any progress. Dwane came out here after about 15-20 years and talked to me. He said he wanted to do some work for me. My wife was sick and I needed someone to do some work for me. I had some of my family come out here and help me with my wife. They came from Atlanta. They wanted to help my wife. What happened was they went home to Georgia to vote for Obama. When they got down there they called me and she said they weren't coming back. She said they wanted money. I sent them $1000 to come and when they got here, they wanted to tell me what to do. They wanted to take over my house. They said I didn't know how to take care of my wife. This time when they went home, I told them not to come back. They had started work upstairs in my house but they didn't finish. So Dwane came around that time and said he wanted to work for me. I told him about my family starting the work and told him he could finish the work upstairs. When Dwane came back after about 20 years, he was in his early 50s. He came out here with four guys. I said well I got to give him another chance. They did the ceiling and did not cover the floor and made a mess. They did a lousy job so I told them not to come back. He put his cousin Glenn in charge after that, but Glenn didn't know what to do. Glenn was a city boy. He never did that kind of work. At that time I gave Dwane my van to go back-and-forth. This way Dwane could get the other people he needed it like a plumber and a guy to put in the lights. They were going to clean up the work that my nephew didn't finish. Dwane knew how to do a bit of work but at that time Dwane was sick. I didn't know that he was sick. Anyway, Dwane and Glenn worked for about two months. They did a lousy job but they completed the job and it was better than nothing. I told Dwane again that I didn't want to be bothered with him. After that Glenn called me up asking me did I have any work to do. What I did was have Glenn come out here and start counting my change, pennies, quarters stuff like that. I had him to wrap up the pennies, anything and then I let him cut the grass. I just had to give him things to do. Glenn stayed with me up until about Christmas. Then we had that big snowstorm in 2014. That's around the time Moses started coming around. Moses helped me with the snow and other things like taking me to the VA. I got rid of Moses like I said. Now somewhere after that time, Dwane sent Priscilla out here. I knew Priscilla's husband when I used to go to the culinary institute. He was going to Yale and we used to walk together. Well, that's how I got working with Priscilla. She was sent here by Dwane. Well, I already talked about that story. Anyway, Dwane came back out here again not too long ago. We start talking and I always liked Dwane, even though he never made any progress. He had an idea about a taxi service and he got a new car. I helped him set up a bank account but he still has not started the taxi service. He has brought me around to the store, the bank and other places. I filled up his tank a few times. I try to help everybody and I am giving him another chance again. He told me he learned from his mistakes but I don't know. He still hasn't got that business going yet. I am giving him another chance. I still like the guy.

Chapter 12
The Man Without A License

In Feb 2015, the Department of Motor Vehicles wanted to test me to see if I was still able to drive. They had me fill out some paperwork at the VA and then they tested me. I ended up having to go for a test two times. I sent two letters two letters to the DMV, Senator Blumenthal and Governor Malloy.

To: The Department Of Motor Vehicles May 20, 2015
cc: Senator Richard Blumenthal
cc: Governor Dannel Malloy

The first letter I wrote said: my name is Jefferson Evans. I was born June 2, 1923. I am almost 92 years old. The VA sent a report of my examination to the DMV. The DMV sent papers to me to have my doctor fill out to see if I was still capable of driving. I was given 30 days to send the papers back to DMV and due to my doctor saying it wasn't his job to do, the papers ending up being late. We also had a hard time getting an appointment with another doctor. The DMV suspended my license at that time which I did not feel was the proper thing to do. That was in February 2015. Finally, I sent the papers in and then I called the DMV to protest suspending my license. I asked them who would I drive until I got an appointment for a test. The DMV send someone to my house the very next day. The person giving the test was named Robert. He asked me to take the test in a vehicle he brought, but I had my own vehicle registered and insured in my driveway. I got in the vehicle and he told me to send the mirrors and he showed me where the signal lights were at. I put my foot on the gas pedal and he started yelling at me, saying the car was warm ready one. I did not know the car was on. I was just feeling around to get used to things. He asked me did I have my license and at that point he took my license. I felt at that point that I was not going to get my license back. I drove safely for me to Stop and S which is about 2 to 3 miles away and stopped in the parking lot. Then he asked me to back up. The chair was too high, so I opened the door to see behind me and he yelled, saying I could not open the door, but I told him I could not see behind me. After that, he told me I had failed. I told him that he did not really give me a chance. I told him he did not explain what he wanted. If you can't see, how are you going to back up without opening the door? He told me to stand up. How are you going to stand up in a car? It was like sitting down in a hole. I think anyone would fail the test if they can't see because the seats are too high……. Sincerely yours, Jefferson Evans the man without a license)

Well, that was the first letter. I told Robert that I thought he was prejudiced. I told him he never gave me a chance. He said, well you think I'm prejudiced. I told him a story about the time the police was in my driveway asking me what am I doing here in Cheshire. I had told those policemen I lived here. He reminded me of those policemen. Then I wrote another letter after my second so-called test.

Sept 7, 2015

To The Dept Of Motor Vehicles:
cc: Governor Dannel P Malloy
cc: Attorney Richard Blumenthal

It read like this: I want to thank the DMV for giving me a second chance at getting my license back. Everyone deserves a second chance. On September 3rd, 2015, you gave me a second chance. I read the paper you sent. You told me to go in my own car or have someone take me. We arrived in Wethersfield, Ct. at 12:00 PM. My daughter brought the papers to the window. They told us to wait for the guy to come back. We waited for about an hour. I sat down in a low chair. At the age of 92, it is hard to get up. I took my time getting up. My daughter saw the guy who weighs about 250 pounds and he was talking, talking, talking. He probably knew I was black and he took about 25 to 30 minutes talking to someone. He came up and said, "are you Jefferson?" I said yes. It took me a while to get up. All I have is time. When we got to the car, he said to get in the car, start the car up and put your foot on the brakes. I did what he said. Then he came to the side of the car window. The car was running, a lot of people were there. He said roll the window down but I did not understand him. He started saying it louder. I got a little nervous and I turned the car off. My daughter had the windows up on the ride there because it was hot and she had the air conditioner on. Well I did not know where the buttons were for the window. They were not on the side near the window where they usually are. They never said on the paper, I was going to have to put the glass down. I did not know that was a required part for driving. I mean using a signal, things like that, I know I would need, but not rolling down the windows. I tried pushing buttons on the panel, but nothing happened. I'm from the south and I remember how white people treated us in the south. When this man started yelling at me, I got nervous, thinking he may do something to me. Then I realized that after the car was off, nothing would work. My daughter said something to him and then he said, "well if he can't turn down the window, he doesn't need a license." My daughter came to the side and tried to show me where the buttons for the window where at, but he yelled at her and told her not to help me. Then he said, "I'm through, I'm through." He didn't give us any paperwork and just walked away. I asked him was he prejudiced? He never gave us any paperwork to say why he never gave me the test. He told my daughter to call someone on the paper I brought, someone named Mary. I have been driving for 75 years. I am not a bum. I am in good shape. I don't know why people treat me this way. Usually, when people treat me badly, they die. I don't know why. He never even gave me a chance. I just want to drive to the store. They took my license even before I took a test. My driving record has been good. This system you have is not good. I think that these white men giving these tests just don't like black men. I feel these guys have been mean. There are some good white people, but these I have come across taking these tests have been mean. Anyway thanks for at least calling me to take the test. I am still, the man without a license. ....Sincerely yours, Jefferson Evans.

I ask the question. **Why do people treat me the way they do?**

Chapter 13
Working The Garden

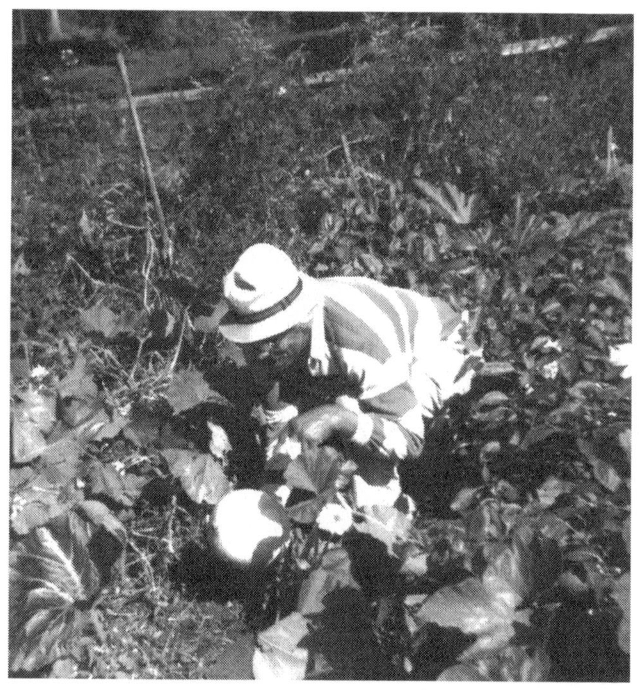

I loved to garden. Near the beginning of April of one year, I remember starting my garden. I plowed my garden. After turning over the soil, I made rows so I could plant different things on each side. Each side of the row is a deep furrow. When I cut the grass, I put grass in the rows in the fall. I even plowed then because it made good soil. In the spring we got a lot of rain. If I did not make the deep furrows the rain would have washed away the soil.

Sometimes I had huge vegetables.

Every year I had a garden. My wife wanted a garden when we first got here. I didn't have time. I was working day and night. She hired somebody to till the garden. Then I started doing everything myself. I had pumpkins. I raised a lot of pumpkins. I used to take them to this guy who had a store in Milford and trade them for food. He told me to bring as many as I could get. Then he said you can have anything out of the store. I remember one year I tried to plant cotton. The winter is too short for cotton so that didn't come out too good. I had such a big garden, one guy said I have a farm out here. I had corn out here that grew four ears to the stalk. My wife didn't know how to fix corn. I took bags of corn down south to Georgia. I stopped in Washington. I gave corn to them. Then I took those bags way down to Georgia. My mother knew how to fix corn. She fixed that corn up. It was so good. I had peppers. I had red peppers, green peppers, yellow peppers. I had all kind of peppers. I never sold anything. I had so many eggplants. I used to sit outside in my van every day and give away vegetables. I had a sign that said free peppers, free corn, free tomatoes. Whatever I had, it was free. People used to come by and they would get it. It looked like they wouldn't come by during the day. They would come at night. They would wait 'til it got dark. Then they would come out. They would come out and take things like the tomatoes and tell me the next day, man, you got some good tomatoes out there. I used to work that garden.

Boy, that was a real garden. I had so many string beans. This guy name Smitty had an old refrigerator and he gave it to me. I used to go out there every morning to pick maybe 5 pounds of string beans. I put them in his freezer and put it down at the greenhouse. I didn't know that freezer was bad. I must of had about 20 pounds of green beans. All of them had rotted in the freezer. I canned tomatoes. I canned apples. I even had an apple tree. A big old red apple tree. I put a wire around it so the squirrels couldn't get in there. One day I went outside and I saw this beautiful red apple. I looked at it I said that is a beauty. I went the next day and that squirrel had put a hole in that wire. That squirrel had got up on that wire and ate that apple. I had pumpkins, zucchini squash. I had a lot of flowers. My wife got mad at me because I gave some flowers away. The flowers I gave away, I was never able to get them again. I never had any more of them. I had beautiful flowers all around the house. The yard was beautiful. I just work, worked, worked. The only thing I didn't grow good was cabbage. Seem like the bugs would eat the cabbage. I grew collard greens, I grew a lot of collard greens. One time I even had strawberries. I had melons, they didn't come out that great, but I have melons. They were cantaloupes. We call them mush melon. You had to put a fence around the garden because this old deer would come there every morning. Seem like he would take his own time and he ate the tops of the tomatoes and then he would go across the road to the neighbors and eat their tomatoes. Then I had these, I think they were groundhogs. They used to eat the tomatoes. They would come up under the fence.

It was a lot of them around here during that time. And they would have babies. One day I saw three of them in the garden. I went up to one and he saw me. I blocked the hole where they came in. I drew back on one and he looked at me and it looked like he start crying, like he said please don't kill me. I just killed him. I killed three that morning. I threw them in the back of the garden in the next day they were gone. The scavengers had come and took them out of there.

One day I came into the house and went into the refrigerator and the water was hot. The refrigerator was eight years old, but I only had insurance on it for five years. A mouse had gotten under the refrigerator and hit the fan. He died but the refrigerator was out. I didn't know who to call. I found the telephone directory and called the first ad that I saw. I told him I need help. My refrigerator is out. He took my name, number and address and came within a few hours. We pulled the refrigerator from the wall and he went to work. he took the screws out from the back and the mouse was under the fan. He gave it to my wife and she had a fit. He wrapped it up in a paper and threw it in the garbage. Anyway I had practically everything in the garden, corn, butter beans, string beans, tomatoes. A guy used to come from New Haven and he picked a whole bucket of string beans. I used to can tomatoes and apples. I went down there after a couple years and they were still good. I used to give away so many tomatoes, boy oh boy. I think that's all over now though. I think this year is my last garden. It's hard now when you can hardly walk to do that kind of stuff. I enjoy doing a garden. I enjoy all this kind of work. I enjoy cooking I enjoy working. I love zucchini squash. They used to grow so big. You have to take care of a garden, keep the weeds down. Mrs. Ford the next-door neighbor, she used to admire how I used to keep the weeds down. Mr. and Mrs. Ford are great. But I don't worry about it anymore. Glenn helped me do the garden for two years. We had a lot of tomatoes. We had some squash, eggplants, green peppers and cucumbers. This year I couldn't help him. He did it by himself, but it wasn't as good this year. Glenn is a city boy, but he learned a little. I couldn't help, my knees wouldn't let me. You get old fast. It seems you're alright one day and the next day you're dead. You get old fast. It seems like it happens overnight. When we were 70, Buni and them thought we were going to die soon. But I'm still here. I'm 93 and I'm still here. I used to love to garden.

Chapter 14

The Presidents

I would like to share a few words about the presidents. I remember back in 1928, The president's name was Hoover. He promised so much that year. When he became president he said everybody would have two cars and a chicken in every pot. Well, when he got in, he put everybody who had a car, the car was in the garage. The pot that was supposed to have chickens in it were empty. That's when the Great Depression came, in 1929. Boy, it was tough. You couldn't even get five dollars for a bail of cotton. That was one president I think my mother voted for, she hated him. That was the worst time we ever had. Hoover was in there from 1928 to '32. My mother had twins in 1932. I was about eight or nine years old then in 1932. After Hoover was in for four years, then Roosevelt got it. The New Deal. He started the country rolling. He started the country moving. He cleaned up the forest. He cleaned up the city. He gave the vets a bonus. But the Republicans always didn't like what he was doing. He put a lot of money out. He built the dam in California. He gave people jobs. Gave people a place to stay. He built railroads. He was sick himself, he couldn't even stand up. His two sons had to hold him up. When he spoke, they were at his side. He got the second term in 1936. Then in 1938, the Germans got the war going. They jumped on Poland. They jumped on France. They just lost the war in 1918. They figured they would try it again. Then they jumped on England. They bombed England every night. In England, there were calling for us, America. The people in America didn't want America to help England. But Roosevelt and Churchill, they got together and America started sending England supplies. At that time there was a lot of prejudice in the United States. It seems like they didn't want the blacks in the army. In 1940 Roosevelt had been in there for eight years. The rule said you could only be president for eight years but the people didn't want to change. The Democrats ruled the house and they kept him in for another four years. In 1941, that's when the Japanese bombed Pearl Harbor. Well, it started a lot of jobs. They were making war guns. They were making planes, ammunition. I think in 1945, that's when Roosevelt died. I was in Washington, D.C. when they bombed Pearl Harbor. I was washing dishes in this restaurant. I was working in a Greek restaurant. Back in those days seem like the Greeks weren't prejudiced. I like the Greeks. They wanted somebody who would work. My father always told us white people don't want slow people. You have to be swift. Well in 1941, we got into the war. They start calling black people into the war. Black people first went to England, then they went to Germany. The people in England hardly seen black people. The white man told them that black people were monkeys. They told him that they had a tail. So the people in England when they saw black people, they said hey, show me your tail. The Japanese, the Germans and the Italians, they were all together. The Italians had taken over Ethiopia. A lot of black people went over to help fight the Italians. After the Japanese bombed Pearl Harbor, well all the Japanese living in places like California, they put them in jail. Everybody in the United States wanted to go fight the Japs. They didn't say anything about Germany, they wanted to fight the Japanese because they bombed Pearl Harbor. When Roosevelt died, Truman became president. Nobody seemed to like him. But Truman is the man, he was from the south and people got mad at him because he was the guy who integrated the army. He put the army together. Truman stayed in for another four years until 1952. Around the same time, people thought this country was going communist. They had what was called McCarthyism. He was Republican. They started locking up a lot of great people. You couldn't even get a job if you looked at a communist. They blacklisted a lot of people in this country. There was a time when you could vote communist. America stopped all that. Even when I move to Cheshire. They said I was a communist. I was with an organization called the I.W.O., the International Workers Organization. The FBI followed me all the way to Germany. You could have a communist card and if you had that card you couldn't even get a job. It was bad. By the time Truman got in in the war was almost over. At that time there was

a guy a general name General MacArthur. I think he wanted to be president. He was a tough guy. He was the guy that everybody loved. He did a lot of great things in the World War II. They put him in command of the Japanese. But he did something, I think that Truman didn't like and Truman fired him. That's when a lot of democrats in the south became republicans. Truman had a daughter who was a singer. People used to say she couldn't sing. He said if you can't stand the heat, get out of the kitchen. Truman was tough. Then Eisenhower became president. Eisenhower was a big guy. He was a Republican. He was the first Republican I am from voting for because he was a soldier. He stayed in for eight years. After Eisenhower in 1960 was Kennedy. Kennedy was from Massachusetts. Kennedy was a big shot. He was rich. He was a senator from Massachusetts. It seemed like Kennedy was more for black people than Eisenhower. Kennedy got killed in 1963. I was living in Cheshire when it happened. Johnson became president after Kennedy because he was the vice president. After Johnson came Nixon. Nixon became the president. Nixon was a tough guy. He was in for a few years. They built this long thing all the way from Alaska to California for oil. Alaska had a lot of oil. We were sending the Japanese a lot of oil. People were saying to Nixon you have to do the right thing. Nixon didn't want to listen to people but after a while, he cut the Japanese off. He didn't send him any more oil. If it hadn't been for Nixon, the Japanese probably would've taken over the country. He was in for a couple years but then Nixon did a lot of bad things. He didn't like what the Democrats were doing. He invaded the Democratic headquarters. This black guy was guarding it and he's the one who turned them in. He saved the Democrats and that's when Nixon got thrown out. That's when Ford got in for a few years because he was the vice president. Then Carter came in, the peanut man. Well nobody seemed to like Carter. They said the peanut man didn't know much. The peanut man did more after he was president then he did when he was the president. His wife cried when he didn't get re-elected after four years. Then the guy from California his name was Reagan. He got in. He was in for eight years. He came in after Carter. People in California didn't like him. My brother said he was a lousy president. After Reagan was Bush, but Bush only stayed in for four years. People didn't seem to like him, but I guess he was all right. Then Clinton came in. He was a Democrat. He stayed in for eight years. He got in trouble with those women but people loved him. After that, Bush's son came in. He stayed in for eight years. The only people that loved him was the Republicans. The Democrats didn't like him. And now the greatest president that I lived under up to now was Obama. He came in '08. It seems like nobody liked him but he is still in. My neighbor across the street, I haven't even talked to him in four years. He said he was a one term president. When he was reelected I went over and said to him, one year president, huh. He said he ain't doing nothing. But all the things he did for the country. He saved the country. Well, it's almost November 2016. We vote for the new president this year. Hillary or Trump. I'm going to vote for Hillary but I bet Glenn a dollar that Trump wins. He says Hillary is gong to win.

Two days before election day, I changed my mind. I decided I would vote for Trump. The people in Connecticut didn't treat me right. All those letters I sent, no-one ever answered me back. I voted for Trump. Trump won. I was right the whole time.

Chapter 15

Day By Day

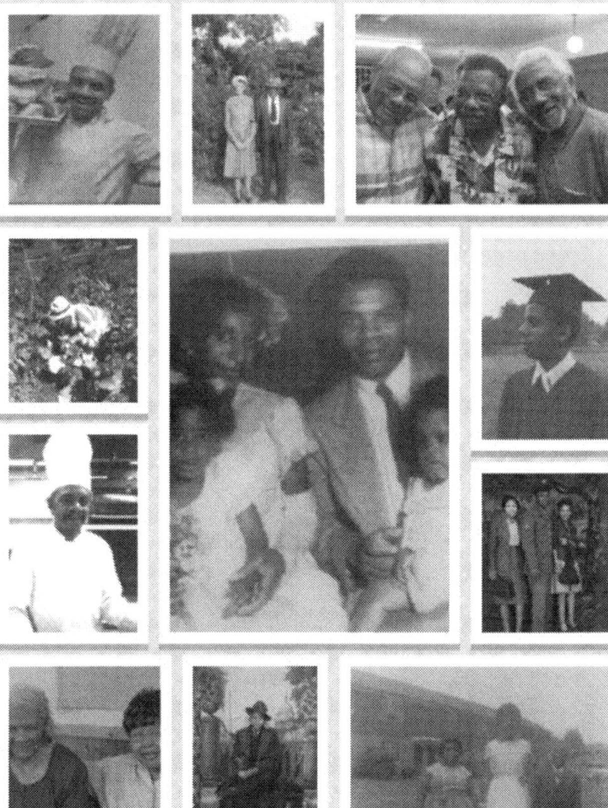

In April 2004, I returned home from Washington DC. I celebrated the home going services for my number one brother, Virtus Evans. His sunset was April 21, 2004 and he was born July 4, 1920. My family went with me. My daughter brought her husband and kids. My brother's wife took it very hard. After taking my brother to the burial ground we came back to the church to have dinner. It was a very long day.

Most of my brothers and sisters are gone. My brothers, Alvin and Burbank are still living and my sister Treat is still alive. I am the oldest.

Here in 2016, I am 93. I am a happy man. I try to eat right. My knees, they are no good. Bones on bones. I can't get around good, but I am a happy man. I cook when I have to cook and I keep busy in the kitchen every day. I have to keep busy doing something. Every now and then about once a week, I get out to the store. Dwane is driving me. I take my time. I ain't got nothing but time. Well, I had to tell you the truth and I know I forgot some things but most of it, it's in here. I'm a happy man. I have been writing this book for over thirty years and now it's done.

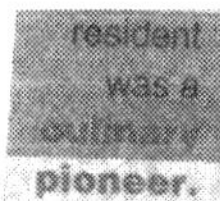

Sunday - April 4th, 2004 CONNE

Institute's 1st black graduate has much to tell in biography

Associated Press

CHESHIRE — Jefferson Evans has packed a lot of history into eight decades. He's trying to get it all down on paper, writing an autobiography — longhand.

"It's pretty hard, you know, when you get to be my age and try to write," Evans says, amid the knickknacks and family pictures in his cozy living room.

He's wearing a blue, red and mostly light-gray warm-up suit. His coarse, silver-white hair is pulled back into a ponytail that his wife, Otelia Evans, doesn't much care for.

"You forget how to spell and your mind runs in different ways," he continues. "You're not like you used to be."

Evan says his next birthday will be 81 (though he also says he's OK with accounts that say he's 82). A Cheshire resident since 1962 and now mostly retired, he still owns and manages a rental property in New Haven. According to Otelia, he can still do yard work with a veagrance.

Jefferson Evan's brush with fame, though, comes from being a pioneer.

He'd intended to go to Yale University after finishing his Army service during World War II — a stint he says was all stateside because of gunshot wounds to both knees that he got from an associate who owed him money and tried to settle up with a gun. It will all be in the book, Evans says.

His mother had been a teacher who had gone to Spelman College in Atlanta, he says. She stressed reading and learning, although the message didn't always get through. Evans' life was rich in other ways.

"My grandfather, he was like a big shot," he says. "Everybody in the South wasn't poor — he had 450 acres of land, my grandfather did."

Evans says he learned how to work hard on that big farm in Georgia.

"My mother used to have a baby this morning, and she was out in the field that afternoon," he says. "We had 12 kids, and it was just one of those things. People were strong."

It's something he carried with him through construction and truck-driving jobs in Washington, D.C., and all the other things he did after coming to Connecticut.

Getting an Ivy League education wasn't one of them.

"I had some nerve to say I was going to Yale," he says.

It's pretty hard, you know, when you get to be my age and try to write."

Jefferson Evans

But the New Haven Restaurant Institute was just opening up, and the GI Bill would pay for Evans to attend that, too.

He gained admittance to what has long since expanded, moved to Hyde Park, N.Y., and changed its name to the Culinary Institute of America.

The school, which says it has an enrollment of 400 students, acknowledges that Evans was its first black graduate, part of the class of '47.

And while racism limited his employment prospects in the 1940s and beyond, Evans says he always made himself indispensable through a series of restaurant jobs by outworking his competition.

He switched jobs a lot, doing construction, painting houses, hauling scrap metal with a buddy and operating his own small tracking line for a time. And in the 1980s Evans ran his own restaurant in New Haven.

"I started out with classy," he says. "And after three days I changed from classy to neighborhood restaurant — pig feet, hot dogs, soul food. I saw that classy stuff wouldn't work."

Before that, in the early 1970s, Evans taught for a couple of years at his alma mater.

He resigned from the Culinary Institute in a dispute over his habit of teaching how to use leftovers — "That's where you really make money, you know, with the leftover food" — but says his students loved him.

Evans' work has been honored by the Black Culinarian Alliance, which in 1995 established a Jefferson Evans Award, which rewards professionalism and creativity within the foodservice industry.

At a recent Black Culinarian Alliance dinner, Luisa Chapman, a 12-year Cheshire resident and co-owner with her husband of a supermarket in West Haven, first realized Evans' accomplishments.

"We've known him ever since we've lived here," she says. "I didn't realize until we were invited to a Black Culinarian Alliance dinner in February, and I'm reading this program and I see there's this Jefferson Evans Award and sure enough, it was him.

"I knew he was a chef, but I didn't know he had done so much."

May God bless you.

Made in the USA
Middletown, DE
24 January 2017